Laughter is Sacred Space

"With the same offbeat lightness and poignant turns that mark his onstage work, Ted Swartz opens the curtain on his own life. Classic Ted. "
—*Carolyn Yoder, author of* The Little Book of Trauma Healing

"Dramatic gift is native to Ted Swartz and he has made good on it in the service of truth-by-humor. This combination of gift and experience makes for a powerful, compelling story."
—*George R. Brunk III, emeritus dean and professor of New Testament, Eastern Mennonite Seminary*

"*Laughter Is Sacred Space* will make you laugh, over and over again! But that's not all—it will captivate you on its spiral journey and will challenge you to think about your own stories of formation. "
—*Joanna Shenk, editor of* Widening the Circle: Experiments in Christian Discipleship

"Ted opens our minds to expansive ways of sharing the good news. Robust faith does not obliterate the pathos of life and death, nor does it eliminate the struggles that constitute our humanity. And Ted reminds us that we can laugh through our tears. "
—*Loren Swartzendruber, president, Eastern Mennonite University*

"Ted speaks of himself as a comic actor, and he is, but he is also a profound preacher. His faithfulness and persistence are compelling. Ted is a modern day icon, pointing people to God with a smile and a chuckle."
—*June Alliman Yoder, professor emerita of communication and preaching, Anabaptist Mennonite Biblical Seminary*

Laughter is Sacred Space

THE NOT-SO-TYPICAL JOURNEY OF A MENNONITE ACTOR

Ted Swartz

First Discarded Subtitle

Mennonite Middle Child—I Don't Expect Much

Second Discarded Subtitle

*A History of Passive-Aggressive Behavior—If You Don't Buy This Book,
I Won't Talk to You*

Herald Press

Harrisonburg, Virginia
Waterloo, Ontario

Library of Congress Cataloging-in-Publication-Data
Swartz, Ted.
  Laughter is sacred space : the not-so-typical journey of a Mennonite actor /
Ted Swartz.
     p. cm.
  ISBN 978-0-8361-9559-0 (hardcover)—ISBN 978-0-8361-9653-5 (pbk.)
1. Swartz, Ted. 2. Actors—United States—Biography. 3. Dramatists,
American—20th century—Biography. I. Title.
  PN2287.S93A3 2012
  791.4302'8092--dc23
  [B]
                              2012020456

For Sue,
who has stood next to me for so long,
through so much,
with grace and strength.

Contents

Foreword

by Brian McLaren

THOUSANDS OF US have seen Ted Swartz perform—solo, with his colleague Lee, or with others.

We've laughed, gasped, winced, and maybe even cried as he ushered us from the sublime, promptly and unceremoniously, to the ridiculous. Or vice versa.

When we've seen actors and comedians onstage (not to mention preachers in-pulpit) we've all wondered what their lives were really like offstage. Is their private persona anything like their public one? (As Ted says, "You cannot fall into the habit of believing in your own public persona, because—believe me—your wife sure doesn't.") So we wonder, when the spotlight flicks off, do the actors transform from clowns to grouches? From exhibitionists to recluses? From beauties to beasts, or artists to jerks?

Tabloids and TV shows sometimes try to raid the privacy of public persons and steal a peak into their personal lives. The result is that public people guard their privacy even more carefully.

Only rarely does an actor or other public figure step off the stage and simply open up as a fellow human being. That's why the book you have in front of you right now is so valuable, so important.

For many years I was a fan of Ted's, sitting in the back row (my favorite place when I'm not on stage myself), smiling and laughing, admiring from a distance. Then some years ago, I had the privilege of getting to know Ted as a friend.

As I read his story, I felt Ted's friendliness shining through. The person I've gotten to know offstage is honestly reflected in these pages.

Ted's honesty is the kind that requires courage. You'll uncover some frank and hard stuff here, much of it left floating in between the lines so you can feel it if you want to, or avoid it if you don't. In that space, there's loss and conflict, and dry spells and sadness. There's depression and death and grief and loss.

And it's all sandwiched between thick slices of whole-wheat laughter. Sometimes it's highbrow, witty laughter. Sometimes … let's just say that Ted isn't above getting a laugh from slapstick, malapropisms, and old-fashioned silliness—down to the level of passing gas or spilling coffee on a sensitive body part.

Somewhere in there, between the sublime and ridiculous, there's "a whole 'nother thing": the profound and poignant. And if you're reading with any degree of consciousness, you'll find a strong dose of that. For example, you'll encounter a hug—an onstage hug that becomes immeasurably significant a few days later, along with the line that precedes it.

And you'll feel moments of anger and hope and downright resilience, too.

If you've got some unhealed wounds, ungrieved losses, or even uncounted blessings (and who doesn't?), reading these pages will be like a good night at the theater. Turning the last page will be like walking across the parking lot after the final curtain and getting in your car.

You won't want to start the car or turn on the radio. You'll just want to sit for a while and let what you've experienced settle in.

A theologian friend recently hit me with a wild proposition: the secular is the domain of the Holy Spirit. "The Spirit was hovering over the surface of the waters in creation," he said, "long before there were any religions or temples or denominations. That's why all of creation—what we call 'the secular'—isn't profane. It's sacred."

Ted knows that. The sacred secular of laughter, tears, joy, pain, tragedy, comedy . . . it's all the stage on which the Spirit plays.

And where we do, too.

—Brian McLaren

Author of *Naked Spirituality* and *A New Kind of Christianity*

Wait, Who's Talking Now?!

A guide to the layout of the book, wherein the author explains to the audience the different voices on the pages—or the voices in his head.

How the book is formatted

1. Classic narrative—the way you would expect books to look.

Dad had a habit of picking through the tomatoes in the produce section. He would find the ones that were "turning bad" and shout, "Yo!" You would turn and find the tomato already in the air; your job was to catch the overripe fruit in such a way as to limit the splash factor. This practice was curtailed for a time after a particularly ripe tomato caught the edge of the meat counter and exploded, a veritable tomato grenade that took the better part of an hour to clean up.

2. Imagined or remembered dialogue—indented. Sometimes whimsical, sometimes factual.

DAD: I guess we should stop doing that for a while.

ME: 'We'? What's with the 'we'?

3. Dialogue from a play or sketch—not to be confused with whimsical, imagined dialogue.

TED: Time was, we could talk and laugh for hours, and NOW I don't even SEE the big picture. It's more like an EXTREME CLOSE-UP of annoyances. You know, if I hear that (*making quotes marks*) "Beatles analogy" one more time I'm gonna scream.

LEE: Take for example Lennon and McCartney.

TED: That's probably what I'll do.

LEE: When they wrote "Love Me Do" it was two people making each other better. But by the time they did *The White Album* it's like just four individuals. It wasn't really THE Beatles anymore, at all . . . you know what I mean?

TED: You get tired of little phrases like "do you know what I mean"?

4. Letters or journal entries—block quote, indented.

From an angry audience member, regarding Ted and Lee taking a crack at the Old Testament:

> I find it repulsive and obnoxious to see the holy God of the Bible reduced to someone who could be acted out in a play. What has Mennonite-ism come to? If Menno Simons were to return from the grave he would surely put the Mennonite church in the same category as he did the Catholic Church in his day. God help us and deliver us from such ungodly influences!

5. Asides appearing as footnotes.

1 I'm an over-packer—especially traveling by van. If you think you might need it, read it, wear it, fix it, by all means throw it in the van.

6. Photos appearing with captions in close proximity to the subject matter.

Ted, at four years old.

How the book is organized

This memoir follows the classic dramatic structure of five acts, preceded by a prologue:

Prologue
ACT 1   Exposition
ACT 2   Rising Action
ACT 3   Climax
ACT 4   Falling Action
ACT 5   Dénouement

Yes, there will be a *prologue* in four scenes, thereby allowing the author to introduce important information necessary in setting up the Classic Five Act Structure. Then, within the acts there are scenes, further illuminating the themes within each act of the Classic Five Act Structure. In addition, there will be *subheads* within each scene, again adding further to the thematic impact illuminated by the Classic Five Act Structure.[1]

---

1 Don't get me started on the asides . . .

Prologue

Wherein the author introduces the audience to the complex relationships between themselves and the performance they are about to view. Here the author may present a dilemma and drop hints as to the possible outcomes.

Beginning in the Middle: A Pivotal Decision

Harrisonburg, Virginia
Spring 1991

THIRTY-SEVEN PERCENT.

Thirty-seven percent is a comfortable humidity level, a great batting average if you're a baseball player. If it's a grade on a test, it is not . . . so great.

I was in seminary, training to be a pastor, and I had failed Greek Exegesis class. Not just failed, actually; obliterated might be a better description. Yes, obliterated, decimated, demolished, pulled a 37 percent on the final. Out of 100, yes.[2]

When people talk of having a calling, we occasionally lift our eyebrows, as if they are telling us they hear voices, including the voice of God, perhaps.

And we mistrust them, these folks who hear voices. Because sometimes a calling is an excuse for selfishness, an abuse of power, and a sense of superiority.

But it's also a powerful thing: it can shape a career, give meaning to life, clarify direction. I had thought I had one—what happened to it . . . this calling to be in seminary, to be a pastor?

---

2   I could never understand why seminaries had you study how to parse Greek verbs to better understand how to lead, inspire, or console a congregation. I understand intellectually why, yes: to have the skills to go into the language in which the texts were originally written, to glean a nugget of original intent, to shine a light to a hungry audience. But language-parsing skills seemed a lot like learning bat making in order to play baseball. Okay, that's off my chest.

I was thirty-two years old, married for thirteen years to my high school sweetheart; I had three beautiful sons (eight, six, and four years old), and a congregation in Pennsylvania counting on me to be a pastor. Not just counting on, but paying for five years of tuition and housing—a recognition and investment in the gifts they had discerned in me. It seemed like a well-orchestrated, God-directed plan, drenched in much prayer and great intentions. In my mind and many others, serving, ministering, pastoring a church was the highest call.

Was it possible to fail a calling?

I hadn't told the congregation about this semester's report card, wasn't anxious for that particular conversation. They hadn't invested thousands of hard-earned dollars for a 37 in Greek Exegesis . . . or a 70 . . . or an 85, quite frankly. My wife, Sue, and I were products of the Swiss German Mennonite community of eastern Pennsylvania. One of the hallmarks of this community was hard work (neat lawns, good business sense) and God's subsequent reward for that effort. This wasn't the plan—failing Greek—and I wasn't wild about the daunting prospect of Hebrew or systematic theology, on the plate for the fall semester. Oh, and what I really wanted? To be an actor.

Tattered calling in hand, I made an appointment with the dean of the seminary, George Brunk—the Third. George was, in addition to being the dean, also the Greek professor, the one who scribbled the 37 across the top of my pitiful attempt at exegeting the book of John. G. B. III is a daunting figure—tall, gaunt, a voice off the bottom of the scale—with an unmatched pedigree in the Mennonite church: son of the most famous, or infamous, evangelist of the 1950s, depending how you feel about coercion and guilt used to ensure a commitment for the Lord.

But George the Third was of a gentler sort. Maybe that's why I wasn't scared spitless, after my first year of seminary, to ask if I could attend advanced acting classes across town at James Madison University, and, in addition, if he would give me credit for those classes.

I was sure this request was the first of its kind. George was either highly prescient or perhaps knew I needed those classes to even keep me in the seminary program. He might have thought, "Let him go, get it out of his system, and we might still have a viable pastoral candidate." He certainly knew I was not a burgeoning Greek scholar.

He said yes.

♕ ♕ ♕

Where the heck was the dang continuing education office? I found myself on James Madison's campus, sixteen times larger than the tiny campus of Eastern Mennonite University, looking for the . . . dang continuing education office.

As a graduate student, I needed a special dispensation from the acting professor at Madison. Because it was an undergraduate class, I needed to register at the continuing education office, which was in a cottage at the other end of campus. I had ridden a borrowed bike with a low back tire, and by the time I had found the correct forms I had missed my appointment time with Dr. Tom Arthur, head of the acting program at JMU. Maybe I should just go home? But I still needed his permission to attend classes. I had come this far. I had kicked one calling to the curb; it probably wasn't the time to give up on the next one.

I went to his office and knocked on the open door. The room looked like I imagined a theater professor's office should—stacks of plays, shelves of textbooks, biographies of the famous and not so famous.

"Dr. Arthur?"

He glanced up. "Yes?"

"I'm Ted Swartz."

(Theatrical pause.)

"You're late."

Should I tell him about the borrowed bike with the low back tire? The fact that the continuing ed. building was approximately thirty-six miles from his office? That it took more guts than I thought I had to even be here!?

No.

"Right. I'm sorry."

"Roger says you're pretty good."

Roger was his colleague who had judged a performance of mine the previous year at Eastern Mennonite and had nominated me for an acting award. Thank God for Roger.

"Okay. . . . That was nice of him."

(Theatrical pause.)

"We'll see."

I think that's a yes.

Thanks, Tom.

❦ ❦ ❦

First day of class: me and twenty-three actual non-Mennonite college students with varying degrees of ability, attractiveness, soberness, and interest. Tom's first words to the class were, "I'm nuts about acting."

I like him . . . I think.

"I'm not sure why, but some students think I'm mean, intimidating, and unfair. I don't think that's true; I just don't like bad acting."

Nice, I'm going to be eviscerated in front of people I don't know.

It was a different class than I had experienced to that point. I had grown to love acting and theater under the teaching of Barbra Graber at Eastern Mennonite. Barbra had just finished her masters in fine arts at the University of Southern California, and was rooted in emotional connections to sense memory, the body, and where the subconscious can lead actors. It was Barbra who initially embodied for me the connection to whole being and art, the idea that artists cannot separate the art from spirit and soul.

However, in Tom's class, we didn't do warm-ups, we didn't learn how to breathe and connect our bodies to the words, we didn't lie down and imagine ourselves in the scene, we didn't bring in our dreams and act them out, we didn't try to dredge up trauma from our pasts in order to create real emotion. We were expected to already know all of those building blocks. We were going to jump into scene work—a little like throwing a child into a pool to teach them to swim.

"I've given you scenes that will push you, and I'm especially happy"—now pointing at me sitting in the second row against the wall trying not to look Mennonite and married—"with what I did to you."

Great.

My scene was from *Entertaining Mr. Sloane*, an English dark comedy by Joe Orton, described in the press like this: "Murder, homosexuality, nymphomania, and sadism are among the themes of this black comedy focusing on a brother and sister who become involved with a young, sexy, amoral drifter with a mysterious past."

Wow. For someone who married their high school sweetheart, never smoked, never drank, didn't curse, this would be . . . interesting.

I would be playing said young, sexy, amoral drifter; I didn't feel I was typecast in any of those descriptions. Compared to the other students, I wasn't young, certainly didn't see myself as sexy, I thought my morals were . . . moral. But I supposed I could drift, if called to.

What was he expecting me to do? Rebel against the theme, the sexuality, the language? Resist his choice of acting partner, a twenty-year-old college student named Mel (short for Melody, not Melvin)?

So I accepted his challenge—and tried to tap into my inner amorality and driftedness.[3]

I jumped in, anxious to prove myself outside of the cloistered world of my Mennonite community. During a rehearsal, the class assistant, Dan, pulled me aside and said, "At the top of the scene, when Mel's showing you the place, grab her and kiss her."

"Kiss her how?"

"What do you mean, how?"

---

3 Most actors will tell you the most fun characters are the bad guys—especially if they are written with nuance. You can then try to compel the audience to like you, confusing their sensibilities.

"Yes, in what . . . manner should I kiss her?"

"You're kidding, right?"

"No."

"You've kissed a woman?"

"Yes, of course."

"That's how."

"Just kiss her?"

"Yes."

"Why would I do that?"

"I don't understand."

"What's the motivation for kissing her?"

(Pause.)

"It's just an idea. Don't you want to kiss her?"

"I didn't say that."

"So kiss her."

"Right."

What he didn't know: I was seriously deficient in experience with women beyond my wife, and I don't know if I was the only one in the room with this experience, but I had kissed exactly one other woman at this point in my life: my wife. Seriously, the only woman I ever dated.[4]

Was this okay—to kiss another woman? Should I write to the board back home at the church in Pennsylvania, who was supporting us? Ask the congregation here in Harrisonburg, where I was serving quarter time on the pastoral team?

Perhaps I should bring it up in ethics class at the seminary. The scene played out in my head, looked like this:

ME: Today in class, instead of manipulating language and ideas to replicate possible scenarios to engender discussion, can I ask the group what they think of me kissing another woman? . . . For the sake of art.

---

4 My dad only ever dated my mom, all three of our sons dated only one woman—in fact, the first time my dad met our youngest son's girlfriend he said, "You know, the Swartzes only date one woman." Not sure that should be the introduction to the first family meeting, but Derek and Chelsea did get married four years later.

THEM: Art?

ME: Yes, acting in a scene.

THEM: Is that art?

ME: Of course.

THEM: I thought it was just pretending.

ME: What?

THEM: Acting.

ME: No . . . is this pertinent to the question?

THEM: You're the one who brought up art. I thought you meant kissing for inspiration to paint.

Or sing.

Or sculpt.

ME: Look, I didn't think I needed to introduce acting as an art form all over again. Can we start over? I've been instructed to kiss a woman in a scene for class.

THEM: Instructed?

ME: Well . . .

THEM: Who instructs someone to kiss a stranger?

ME: Well, she's not really a stranger.

THEM: Even so.

ME: Okay, maybe not instructed, but it was a strong suggestion.

THEM: You said instructed.

ME: Right.

THEM: So you weren't being truthful.

ME: Perhaps I exaggerated to make a point.

THEM: And this is what you are learning at JMU, lying?

ME: No . . .

THEM: This is for acting class?

ME: Yes!!

THEM: Is it necessary for the scene?

ME: I don't know yet. Just trying it out.

THEM: Do we have to try everything out before we can make a moral judgment?

ME: How else can we make decisions?

THEM: Do you have to smoke pot to make a moral decision about it?

ME: What??

THEM: Do you have to have sex with another woman before you say it's not a good idea?

ME: I'm not having sex with . . .

THEM: How does it affect the body?

Yes, good question, how does it affect the body?

ME: My body?

THEM: No, the body of Christ!

I want to know how it affects *his* body!

Christ's?

No, Ted's!

ME: It's just a kiss!!

THEM: Is a kiss ever really just a kiss?

(Theatrical pause.)

ME: How about if I promise not to enjoy it?

Yes, that might have been an interesting ethics class.

I took none of those options. Next rehearsal, when that time came, I "drifted in" and kissed her. Now, unbeknownst to her, Mel had the distinction of being the second woman I had ever kissed in my life. I don't know if I surprised her. I must have: why else would she have given me the tongue?

So now, *she* had surprised *me*.

In an odd sort of way, it was the right thing to do, perhaps; that's what makes acting alive, surprising each other.

I do remember the thought that went through my mind: *God, I wish she didn't smoke.*

That classroom, Experimental Theater 11, was a great laboratory, where we experimented with emotions, voices, bodies, fears, anger . . . it was heavenly. I was in a place where no one knew me; there were no expectations, there was no one watching me for behavior unbefitting a future pastor in the Mennonite church. It was a remarkably clean slate to scribble on. It seemed crucial that I scribble with abandon; I wasn't willing to accept a 37 percent in acting class.

It is somewhat fitting, I think, that the two most important class spaces in my formal acting education were cast-off spaces on their respective campuses. EMU's Guild Theater, where I took my first-ever acting class, was the gym for the college in the 1930s and '40s; later the bottom floor became first the wet art room, then a storage room, and then a maintenance space. In fact, I changed the brake pads on our Toyota there eight years previous to that first acting class, when Sue was an undergrad student there.

At JMU, the acting classroom, room 11, was in the experimental theater, an ex-turkey hatchery. It stank, leaked, and flooded often. The overhead lights were harsh, the furniture shabby, but the space was fiercely defended by students. It too was a great lab for discovering theater.

Tom didn't structure class with a schedule for performances. When he asked, "So, who's ready?" if you *were* ready, you jumped up. However, before you could speak, he would ask, "What do you want in the scene?"

If you paused, he said, "You don't know, sit down." What you wanted had to be something you could act—not an idea, nothing unspecific. How did your "want" translate into action? Because, after all, it *is* acting.

In places like acting laboratories you sometimes discover the best of what you are, and also the worst of what you can be. When actors are free to experiment it can be the most exhilarating place on earth. It can be like falling in love when the creative spirit jumps out of you and begins dancing with the spirits of the others in the scene, when the sparks are almost visible, when you can feel the cords of energy connecting you to your acting partner, when you feel the audience leaning forward, wanting to share in the same energy. When you come off stage and ask, with wonder and awe, "What just happened there? And when can we do it again, feel that again?"

I discovered the mystical and spiritual life for the first time. Theater helped me to see the world of the invisible, showed that forces greater than ourselves are at work and play in the world.

That's why Tom Arthur was "nuts about acting." And why Barbra Graber felt theater and art was a lens through which to view the world. And that's why I fell in love with an art form I had, to this point, admired from afar and only occasionally flirted with.

I had finally found who I was.

I was an actor.

A Leap Forward in Time: Hints of the Crisis in Act 3

Harrisonburg, Virginia
Summer 2010

I'M SITTING IN the bathroom, looking at my underwear, thinking of the prophet Jeremiah.

A favorite character of mine is Jeremiah, from the two-man show I coauthored, *Creation Chronicles*, a comedic tour through the Hebrew Scriptures, or the First Testament in the Christian Bible. In chapter 13, this prophet receives a peculiar instruction from God; the following is paraphrased *only* slightly, in a rural southern dialect:

```
It was a little while back that the Lord says
to me, he says, "Jeremiah"—that's what he
generally calls me, Jeremiah—he says, "Jere-
miah, go buy some shorts . . . and wear these
shorts, but don't worsh 'em." That's what he
said, so that's what I did.

I went and got me a pair of shorts and I wore
'em, but I didn't worsh 'em. I was never that
popular anyway.

And then the Lord says to me, "Jeremiah"—
that's what he generally calls me. "Jer-
emiah," the Lord says to me. "Jeremiah, take
off them shorts."
```

And he said: "Go to Parah and hide dem shorts
in a crack in the big rock." That's what
he said, so that's what I did. I took them
shorts off—pheeeeewwwww!—and I took 'em on
over to Parah and hid dem shorts in a crack
in the big rock.

It was a little while later that the Lord
says to me, "Jeremiah"—that's what he generally calls me, Jeremiah—"Jeremiah, go back
and get dem shorts what was in the crack in
the big rock."

So I went back and dug them shorts out of
that crack what was in the big rock. (*Produces traumatized, astoundingly ragged, filthy
shorts, from his pocket; regards them.*)

Well, they didn't look the same. I didn't
think they would . . .

So I am thinking about Jeremiah . . . and Lee.

Lee Eshleman and I had been acting and creative partners for three months shy of twenty years, creating six full-length theatrical or comedy shows, carving out a business and a full-time living in the performing arts—a task of love, sweat, and determination.

We were exploring life and sacred texts with an eye toward what was askew, peculiar, and above all—where was the funny? Always, what was funny? It was a celebration of laughter as a healing art, a teaching method, an absolute affirmation that humor is a profound and indispensable societal lubricant. Ted & Lee Theater-Works was a combination of business, career, artistic exploration, and love. It was our calling—together.

Until Lee took his own life in 2007.

Now I'm perched on the edge of the tub, eyeing my underwear that is falling apart—holes in the front, holes in the back. I'm creating a holey monument to stubbornness, anger, and resolve—with a dash of self-pity. It's been over three years since Lee died, and I'm working harder than I ever have, scrambling, the business spiraling down, personally spinning wheels, and carrying debt—debt that makes me angry, depressed, and stubborn. The baggage of grief, guilt, and anger would have been enough without adding in debt.

The business collapsed following Lee's death; not unusual when the theater company assets are limited to an inventory of intellectual property, which is in turn coupled to actors with fourteen hours' worth of material filed away in their heads. It was something akin to owning a trucking company with a fleet of trucks suddenly missing all of their right tires.

I resolved to move forward, literally and figuratively.

I wasn't going to go into another line of work. I wasn't going to submit my name for possible pastoral candidates, I wasn't going back to school for another degree in order to teach, I wasn't going to paint houses again, I wasn't going to apply at the local Food Lion as a meat cutter . . . I just wasn't—period. I was an actor.

Several months after Lee died, I had turned around all pictures of Lee in my office and put into storage all T-shirts and clothing with a

"Ted & Lee" logo or name. I had stripped my budget of movies, maga-zines, music, and especially clothes. I had resolved to neither buy nor receive as a gift any piece of clothing until the debt was resolved—debt that was there when Lee died, plus debt that I amassed when I went ahead with a project we had contracted together.

The United Methodist Church publishing house had asked us to produce thirty-two video scenes from the Bible, to connect to a curriculum—a huge undertaking for a tiny three-person com-pany, with two and a quarter employees. It was entitled *Good God Theater*, and ultimately cost a little less than $174,000 to produce.

Unbeknownst to me, the economy was about ready to dive, the market for DVDs going with it. And I had invested personally in the project—$108,000 on credit cards. The sales from the *Good God* project were projected to return investment within two years, according to the most conservative projection from the publisher. Ultimately the products sold about one-fifth of that low projection, so I was left with the debt when Lee died. Angry with Lee, I "told" him that his pictures would face the front when I was debt free.

Now, three years later, it might seem strange to someone walk-ing into my office to see absolutely no indication of the man who was such a part of my life for twenty years.

The "no new clothes" rule is a little harder to explain. I think it's probably along the lines of a hair shirt, a sign of self-sacrifice. It was a symbol, a sign. "The clothes will fall off my body before I give in to you." A tangible way to put a handle on my grief, anger, and resolve.

Well, after three years it's taking longer than I thought it might. And my stubbornness is getting on my wife's nerves. When I am down to the really ratty underwear that week, I dress when she's not around, or scrabble sideways, so as to not give her a view of my back-side—sort of like an actor who's been told to always face the audi-ence. Am I thinking I have fooled her, her, top of the class, master educator, president of our high school's National Honor Society?

My own shorts now look almost as bad as Jeremiah's. And, another line from Jeremiah comes to mind: "It's hell bein' a walkin' metaphor."

Is that what I've made myself? A walking metaphor?

A Leap Back in Time: Critical Elements That Will Affect Later Decisions

Spring City, Pennsylvania
Fall 1974

THE YEAR I GRADUATED from high school, I was at work in the family butcher shop Tuesday afternoon, when the phone rang. I picked it up.

"Hello, Swartz's."

"Ted, it's Duane."

"Hey."

"Just wanted to let you know a group of us are going over to the Bishops' tomorrow night."

"Okay . . . why?"

(There was a pause.)

"To be with Greg's parents."

(Now my turn to pause.)

"Why?"

"He was killed last night; didn't you know?"

I was now sliding down the wall, my bloody meat-cutting apron dragging the floor, crying, all the stupid things we worry about when we're seventeen now unimportant, the Hatfield Meats hat crumpled in my fist.

Greg Bishop, member of the class of '74, was killed in a single car accident Monday, no alcohol involved, just new blacktop, a higher road shoulder, and a car with too much horsepower. Too many of us had those kind of cars. I had a '70 Chevelle with a 454 cubic inch engine; three other classmates had the Chevelle, another a Camaro. Greg drove a green Charger.

For those of us who didn't go to college, the rural roads of eastern Pennsylvania were the playgrounds of teenagers with cheap gas and big engines. My top end was probably around 130 to 135 miles an hour—and I do remember the last time I hit 120. It was just up the road from The R, the all-night restaurant where we gathered, a pack of muscle cars spinning out of the parking lot, tires squealing, going north on the 309. While I was never a serious car head and never as reckless as others, we all loved the speed and the sound of those engines. As I hit 120 that night, I thought, *My right front tire is wearing bald; if it blows, I'm dead.* I slowed down and never drove that fast again.

I had spent the night at Greg's Sunday night; his folks, Russ and Rhoda, were out of town. A group played tackle football Sunday afternoon and Greg lent me clothes to play in. A pair of jeans and a flannel shirt . . . Sue and I still have the flannel shirt.

Wednesday night we went over to the Bishops', who had come home from Colorado to the sight of police at their door, bearing the news of Greg's death.

Now the house was full of people, lots of adults Russ and Rhoda's age, speaking in hushed tones, trying to discern the right thing to say. The seventeen- and eighteen-year-olds gathered in a section of the living room and talked about Greg. We soon found Russ and Rhoda with us, because in their great pain, they wanted to hear us talk about their son, to hear us describe his cackling laugh, his wiry, seemingly unbreakable body, his great guitar playing, his astonishing ability to grow facial hair. Kids just trying to stay attached to memories of a beloved friend.

That Sunday night a group went back over to the Bishops' on Cherry Lane. We needed each other; it was a good place to gather—a sacred place, although we didn't know that then. In our stumbling, immature ways we were doing for the Bishops what they also needed. No one determined a plan, but we just kept going back each Sunday night, sometimes as few as three, sometimes closer to thirty. If they had church that Sunday night, we just waited until 9:30. We needed those gatherings to hear each other, touch each other, see each other. The illusion of indestructibility among youth had been shattered; those gatherings gave us back some of the sense that we would live, if not forever, for a time longer. So we kept going back. And going back. For two and a half years, we gathered at the Bishop house.

It was, in many ways, the best thing I was a part of. It was remarkable, given we didn't know what we were doing—embracing the best of what community has to offer, alleviating some of the pain for Greg's folks, even while we were trying to make sense of our loss.

Sometimes the best kind of God-work happens when you don't know what you're doing.

A Critical Character Reintroduced: The Tall One, the Funny One

Harrisonburg, Virginia
Fall 1987

BEFORE SUE AND I left Pennsylvania for my first year at Eastern Mennonite University, I had been asked to write and perform a number of sketches for a youth leaders' retreat at Spruce Lake, a Mennonite camp in Canadensis, Pennsylvania. The theme was peace and justice; could I write sketches to introduce the main sessions around the theme, and could they be funny?

I prepared the pieces at EMU, early that fall. The pieces I wrote included characters based on a classic Monty Python sketch, "The Spanish Inquisition."[5] Craig Sottolano, an incoming first-year student at EMU, had agreed to work with me, so I wrote the pieces based on our particular abilities and types.

The retreat weekend was soon upon us. Our plan was to stop at my folks' home in Spring City, Pennsylvania, drop off our two older boys, and continue on up to Spruce Lake. Derek wasn't yet six months old; Sue was still nursing him, so he had to go along.

The Monday before, Craig called me and said the director of the fall production, *A Midsummer Night's Dream*, had called a rehearsal for the weekend.

---

5 All comedic writers steal ideas and concepts constantly; the roots of comedy are ultimately all connected.

He couldn't go.

So I was stuck. I spent two days calling anyone I could think of who had the interest and ability. After striking out with that approach, I jettisoned the ability part and just went with "anyone with interest."

Still no luck.

I was sitting in EMU's Campus Center when Joe Lapp, the new college president, happened by. As a joke—I think—I asked, "Joe, would you like to go to Spruce Lake with me and perform for the weekend?"

He said no, thankfully. Joe might have been a fine college president and lawyer, but an actor, he's . . . a fine college president and lawyer.

However, he did say, "What about Lee Eshleman?"

"I've seen him; he's funny—but I've never met him."

"I'll introduce you."

So I followed Joe into the print shop where Lee was working. He worked part-time there and also part-time as the graphic designer for the college.

Joe said, "Lee Eshleman, meet Ted. Ted Swartz, meet Lee. I think you two have something to talk about." And then he left.

"Hello."

"Hello."

"Well, um . . . I . . . You don't know me."

"Right."

"But I've seen you onstage."

"Okay."

"At the inauguration comedy show."

In the background, the copy machines churned out some publication crucial for the movement of the university.

"Good."

"Funny."

"Good. Thanks."

I opened my briefcase and showed Lee what I had in mind.

"There isn't any money, but it's a beautiful camp, and there's a very good chance we'll have a lot of fun."

He said he would have to think about it.

Later, he told me it was probably the desperate look in my eye, and the fact that I had based these pieces on the Monty Python routine, that made him even listen. I was to find out this was very atypical of Lee—to take a chance on the unknown.

That was Wednesday. Later that night he called me and said yes, he would go. Thursday evening we talked through the sketches. I had to rewrite them, because Lee was going to play the role I had written for me, and I was going to play Craig's role. Lee played higher status better than I did: he was taller, good-looking, had a great voice and an aristocratic nature that he conveyed easily onstage. I played the rougher roles, the dirtier roles, the ones you might say were . . . less intelligent.

And so, Friday morning, Lee hopped in the van with Sue, me, and the three boys. On the way we rehearsed the first piece to be performed that night. We were the *Obmar Patriot Patrol*. Obmar is Rambo[6] spelled backwards; the sketch was an attempt to take the issues of war, aggression, and violence and turn them around.

At the retreat, we were introduced by Jesse Glick, who had hired us—I mean, who provided food and lodging. As he announced the next session we waited for the lines, "Following the afternoon workshops there will be time for response to the speaker, some free time . . . and of course, we *don't* expect the Obmar Patriot Patrol."

We burst in screaming, "No one expects the Obmar Patriot Patrol!!"

"Our chief weapon is fear . . . and ignorance."

"Our two chief weapons are fear and ignorance . . . and a blind nationalism."

"Three!!! Our three chief weapons are fear and ignorance and a blind nationalism . . . and a fundamental belief that God is from Ohio."

"Four!!!! Amongst our weaponry are such diverse elements as

---

6 *Rambo*: the film with Sly Stallone, who plays a violent, monosyllabic character. No, that's not what Stallone always played.

fear and ignorance, a blind nationalism, and a fundamental belief that God is from Ohio. How do you plead?!!?"

Lee was brilliant. He made everyone laugh; he sure made me laugh. We had comfortably found a format that would work over and over again—me the dense one, he the smart one. People thought we'd been working together for years, when in reality we had met just three days before. It was magical. It was spiritual. It was more fun than I'd ever had onstage.

We had each found our comedic soul mates.

One day, the new math teacher at the high school where Sue teaches put eight old photographs in Sue's mailbox. Someone at the teacher's previous church in Pennsylvania had found them while cleaning out a file. They were from the first weekend that Lee and I spent together. Pat Robertson was running for president that fall, hence the "Vote for Pot/Pat" on the bedpan. See, *pot* refers to the bedpan, not the stuff you smoke. Whether or not you believe a bedpan was appropriate for Pat's presidential platform is up to you.

❝ ❝ ❝

For the next couple of years while I attended college and then seminary, Lee and I performed occasionally, developing material around invitations to retreats and events on campus. For the first few shows we borrowed material, then gradually developed our own. Out of those times, along with simple activities—eating together, listening to music—we became fast friends.

He became part our lives. The boys now had an eccentric uncle who made them laugh, taught them songs, gave them nicknames: Peanut Butter and Jeliot (Eliot), Ian the Human Bein', and Derek von Schterick, the world's loudest tuba player (an homage to Don Martin of *MAD Magazine* fame). He helped with their care on more than one occasion, babysat, and wove himself into the fabric of our family. "Looks at Books," a sketch which debuted our most identified comedy characters, was developed and fleshed out while he was helping me give the younger boys a bath. The boys never knew life without Lee.

Within two years of meeting Lee however, we began to witness his struggles with depression. It was our first encounter with a clinically diagnosed illness up close. When I would veer through the campus center on my way to seminary and stop in to see him at work, I was never sure exactly which version of Lee I would find. Would it be the one who, in the throes of a manic stage, was ready to take over the communications department, or the one who would simply look up from his desk when I came around the corner, despair pooling in his huge blue eyes?

In late 1990, the depression reached a desperate point and he was hospitalized. He moved to a psychiatric facility in Maryland and the future of our partnership was in question.

Act 1

Exposition

Wherein background information enables understanding of how an actor might develop out of the environment of a cloistered religious community, work for fifteen years as a meat cutter, then attend seminary with intent to become a pastor.

SCENE 1

Family, Church, and Baseball: The Value of Inadvertent Theater Training

Spring City, Pennsylvania

Family—safety, nightmares, and birth order

So how does a Mennonite from rural Spring City, Pennsylvania, end up an actor, testing the murky, unprofitable waters of art and theater, looking for place? It might help to define why so many of us are drawn to theater.

At its best, theater embraces a sense of community and—albeit temporarily—creates a family. At the end of a show's run, you should prepare for a sense of mourning. The character you have created is no more; it's as if he or she is dead. There is also a loss of relationship; your family is gone. Many of us who have fallen in love with theater are drawn to this sense of family and place. Acting cannot be practiced alone.

During rehearsal and performance, actors give themselves to each other in a way that is often more intense than normal life. Exposing yourself to hundreds of people every night is hard, scary; it should be done in the company of people who care for you fully.

❧ ❧ ❧

This photo illustrates many of my perceptions of childhood. I'm on the right, and holding my hand is my older brother, Tim—my best friend, leader, and protector. Our grandmother Nana, who lived next door, has her large, meaty arms around us both, a warm, enveloping presence. Her name was Grace and she embodied her name. The large head covering is a nice touch.

Tim is sixteen months older than me, and like many second sons growing up with an older brother that close in age, I followed every directive from him. But it seemed to go a bit beyond that.

Once a week Mom did the wash, including bed sheets. She had us make our own beds, with the hospital corners. After I made mine, I would make Tim's bed as well. For some reason I thought I would score a few points if I made my bed and then his. In the winter when the sheets were cold I would sometimes warm up his bed for him. It seems, in retrospect, going way above and beyond the call of duty for second sons.

When we worked at our parents' grocery store, doing odd jobs for a couple of dollars, we would pool our money to buy a new model car . . . for Tim to put together. Perhaps it was an investment—but it was *his* model car. I know, because when he would make me angry, it was his models I would surreptitiously break small parts off of. Yes, the same models I helped purchase.

It's the second sons whose tasks are often clearly defined. One time, for instance, when attempting the great Zorro move of riding underneath a tree and grabbing a branch to swing up into the tree, thereby eluding the pursuit of the hapless soldiers of the Spanish government—it was the *older* brother who would approximate the hero, while the younger's job entailed catching the suddenly riderless bicycle. The maple tree beside the driveway was deemed the best possible tree for the attempt. The approach was smooth. Tim reached up to grab the branch, accomplished the "dismount" as the bike stayed on track, and I braced myself and made a grab for the handlebars . . .

. . . and the bike fender drove right into my knee.

Mom[7] was a nurse, so we didn't go to the doctor for minor injuries—scrapes, cuts, concussions, or a bike fender embedded in a knee. Slap a Band-Aid on it, apply some antiseptic Mercurochrome, and back out to play. No stitches necessary.

Tim and I are very clearly brothers, but also very different. Tim never seems to get angry, is always calm when I can be volatile. He's the meticulous visual artist who can stay in front of the canvas for hours, while I'm the ADHD candidate—oh look, the mail just arrived—whose art form includes the great need of performing in front of people.

As all brothers do, Tim and I fought. But there was an unwritten rule about fists: punching above the shoulder was forbidden. He would laugh when I got frustrated and angry and punched away at his mid-section and chest. Of course that laughter made it worse.

The "never above the shoulder" rule lasted until I was four-

7 Mom was also the unofficial community nurse for a number of cousins. I have this vivid image of an entire family of five children, having come to our place for shots, all leaning forward over the back of the couch with their pants around their ankles. Mom just worked her way down the line—naked bottom—*boink*—after naked bottom—*boink*—after naked bottom—*boink* . . .

teen, on a winter weekend when we were sledding at Spruce Lake Camp. We had a disagreement—probably about whose turn it was for the sled—and we began wrestling. And then . . . he hit me in the mouth. I was hurt mostly because of this clear breach of etiquette. He hit me in the mouth!

Recently, when we remembered that great faux pas, he commented,

"I had to hit you in the mouth."

"Why?"

"I couldn't breathe."

Oh. I must've been winning. I hadn't thought of that. Usually when we fought, a formal apology did not follow. One or the other would just ask, "Do you want to throw?" And we would grab our gloves and head outside.

Tim was also my first collaborator in discerning what was funny—we were drawn to the comic. We didn't put shows together, practice magic tricks, or act in plays while young. But we always had our antennae up for the funny.

Because we didn't own a television while growing up, whenever we visited friends or relatives who did, we were, naturally, entranced by the "demon box." Once while visiting cousins who had a TV we stumbled upon a movie our parents would never have let us watch, had they known. It was Vincent Price's *The Fly*. And it scared the living crap out of us. In the film a man develops a machine which transmits the molecules of animate objects from one physical space to another. The ultimate test of course, was to transmit a human being. But when the scientist stepped into the machine, unbeknownst to him, a fly entered the machine as well and so he stepped out of the machine half man, half fly. His head was now the fly's head—a remarkable bit of '50s horror genre.

I asked Tim if I could sleep with him that night and every night for the next three weeks. Even though my bed was right next to his, it felt safer to actually be under the covers with someone else. My imagination was nearly as good as the nightmares that came somewhat naturally to me. Mom tells the story often of waking up with this sense of a looming presence in the room, to find me just standing there beside the bed. I wouldn't want to wake her; I would just stand there, wishing-hoping that someone would make it all okay. Then she would take me back to bed.

I did suffer from actual nightmares, but some of it was just an enthusiastic imagination. Tim got tired of me asking if he would share his bed with me to alleviate my nightmares and fears, so I asked my sister Tina if I could sleep with her. This worked well, as she was actually looking for the opportunity to alleviate her own nightmares and fears.

About ten years ago Lee and I found ourselves in a hotel room with the afternoon off and while surfing the TV channels discovered the original *The Fly*. So we watched it. It was almost as frightening as I remembered when I was ten. So that evening I called my sister Tina.

"Hello."

"It's Ted."

"Hi."

(Pause.)

"Are you okay?"

"I don't think so."

"What's wrong?"

"I watched *The Fly* this afternoon."

(Much laughter.)

"Okay."

"Yeah . . . so . . . can I sleep with you tonight?"

(More laughing.)

"I'll have to check with Jay . . . to see if there's room in the bed."

I sometimes describe my birth order position as akin to sitting in a rocking chair or a hammock. To me, it seemed safe and protected without angst or psychological damage. Tim, the oldest, and Tina, the youngest, seemed to have issues that I didn't have.[8]

---

8 When Tina found out I was writing a book she said, "I get the last chapter because you have no idea what it was really like."

At around sixteen, it seemed Tim abdicated the eldership to me. Perhaps because he felt disconnected from Dad, I became the more responsible son, the one who stayed home to work in the family business, who lent money to Tim while he went off to discover the world. I was married first, by six years, and first to be a father. It seemed I was the older son until we reached our forties and the tide seemed to flow back to the natural order. I was the middle child again—a welcome change.

Sitting in a room at a conference last year—three siblings together without spouses for the first time in decades—amid a group of friends, someone asked, "So who's the oldest?"

I thought he was joking. Tim, while in possession of all of his hair, is grayer than I am, and his beard and eyebrows are silvered, while my eyebrows have remained dark. I thought it was obvious who was the oldest, because Tina . . . well, she's the youngest, the little one, the girl tagging behind.

So I asked, "Who do *you* think is the oldest?"

He didn't hesitate.

"Tina."

Ted, Tina, and Tim as children.

Tim, Tina, Ted at nephew Jordan and Gina's wedding. Tina and I wrapped around each other; Tim, arms folded, a comfortable space between us. We are all happy, grinning at the end of a wonderful day of celebration . . . but staying where our comfort zones would take us.

"Really? Why? To me she doesn't look anything close to the oldest."

"She acts older."

Ah, so the actor and the artist, the baseball nuts, the ones who still have a coded language of grunts and chuckles—they don't act as responsible as the social worker in charge of placements for foster children in one of the largest faith-based agencies in the city of Philadelphia. Is that what you're saying?

Yes?

Okay, just so I'm clear.

Church: learning sacred space, the roles of the performer and audience, and passing gas

The Mennonite Church was a huge part of our lives, often involving three services a week: two on Sundays and usually a Wednesday night service. Church wasn't just something you did on those occasions; your life was supposed to reflect your commitment throughout the week. For many of us, the structure of church is where we learned ritual and presentation, and the order of service (the program, indicating how to respond as congregation or audience).

In the 1950s my parents joined a mission church in Pottstown, Pennsylvania. A number of such churches were started in the '40s and '50s in that part of the country. Well-intentioned rural Mennos traveled into "needy" urban areas to plant churches—a model that in retrospect seems akin to planting seeds in shallow soil, or perhaps planting seeds in a field you don't have plans to visit more than once a week.

For us kids, it was a comfortable place. We learned the Bible stories. We read books about intrepid missionaries with titles like *Man Eaters Don't Lie*—complete with a very enticing drawing of a ferocious lion.

And yes, we had flannelgraphs. If you are of the video age, you probably missed flannelgraphs—children gathered at the front of the church, sitting on the floor in rapt attention as a woman told a story, usually from the Bible, illustrated with figures affixed to a sheet of flannel. It was theater at the basic level: the hand moved smoothly in conjunction to the story, the bottom of the felt figure placed first and then a smoothing upward motion to make it stick.[9] I think the appeal was in the anticipation of "what's next?" It was a story visibly unfolding.

A Sunday morning usually started with Dad in the car, parked sideways in the drive, ready; Mom, her covering affixed properly to her head . . .

"What is a covering?" you might ask. Women, according to the apostle Paul, were to keep their heads covered. By this period in our stream of Mennonite history, the earlier style of the bonnet had been reduced to a dainty piece of lace material perched atop the head. This now passed as a "covering." The covering didn't really

---

9   I wonder if they received special training on "flanneling." This week: "Tightening up those pregnant pauses."

cover much anymore; it was symbolic. Sometimes the women who only wore coverings for church would simply pin them to the ceiling of the car after church, and there the coverings would wait until the next time, hovering like halos of perceived virtue.

I have strong memories of supper time, Mom hollering for someone to get her covering for supper prayer, me racing back to the bedroom, reaching high to retrieve it off the dresser, and then wearing it back to the kitchen—a mild form of cross-dressing, I suppose.

Why did we have coverings? Did we always have coverings? During the revivals in our version of the Swiss German Mennonite Church in the early twentieth century, the church adopted a strict dress code, creating interesting fashion designs in the effort to be uniformly "plain." The men wore a "straight coat," without lapels— way ahead of the Nehru jacket of the '60s—and either no tie or, in some cases, a bow tie.

The women wore the head coverings plus "cape dresses," another symbolic, created fashion. A piece of fabric was sewn onto the front of the dress to create another layer of modesty. Not only were the breasts hidden, they were additionally layered—sort of a "double knot" against the threat of lustful thought. That didn't— and still doesn't—stop young women from wearing the first *and* second layer as tightly as possible. More aerodynamic, I suppose, for speed in walking.

In ninth grade Christian Living class at Christopher Dock High School, the teacher described the practice to us, in painfully graphic language. "In Lancaster County," he told us, his voice quivering, "the girls purposefully—purposefully, mind you—wear dresses cut to . . . accentuate[10] rather than to *hide* the breasts." And then he wept.

We were stunned—that he wept; that he said *breasts*; and, quite frankly, as soon as he said "breasts in tight dresses," we—the boys—were gone.

---

10 The word *accentuate* retains, to this day, a vague connotation of titillation.

If you tended toward the hefty side like my Nana, the extra material necessary to create a cape to cover an ample bosom created a sort of kangaroo pouch where hankies, important papers, and, occasionally, candy could be stored.

My parents participated in both fashions during their twenties and thirties. When Dad stopped wearing his plain coat in the 1950s, he was told by a member of the congregation, "You are going down"—unless he straightened up. We assumed "going down" meant hell. We were pretty sure he wasn't going to deck Dad. Good Mennonites didn't hit anyone. Damning them to hell was much cleaner, and somehow sanctified.

My great-grandparents in 1897.

My parents in 1953. At Mom and Dad's wedding, there was no choir allowed in the conservative Lancaster County Mennonite church where they were married. There would certainly not have been instruments either, so the only music allowed was typical hymn singing by the congregation. So Mom and Dad chose six of their best friends who sang well and gave them the music to several songs—the only ones with music, they became ostensibly a choir. Nice job, Mom; subversive wedding planning.

❦ ❦ ❦

Where was I? Ah, in the car on the way to church. Mom, checking for spots on our faces and upon finding them, applying the dreaded spit bath: she'd lick a hanky and scrub at our faces. I remember the smell of coffee and a strong aversion to this practice.

We were headed for Prospect and Hanover, to our brick, sturdy, *plain* church building, 120 on the attendance roll. That number didn't change for years. Oh, there was fluctuation, but for some reason the number seemed nailed to the board—I guess *any* kind of change was akin to moral failure. Or perhaps no one was interested in checking if those who were members still *wanted* to be members, whether or not they'd graced that space in the last decade.

Once you were in your unpadded pew, you didn't leave; no bathroom breaks, no drink breaks. No toy trucks were allowed—but maybe the Scotty magnets: two dog magnets, one black, one white.

"You'd put one under a piece of paper, the other on top, and then move the bottom one—magically, the top dog moved!"

"Cool, so what else could you do with them?"

"Well, ah . . . see . . . you put the black one under the paper . . . you can't see it. Then you put the white one on top."

"Does it have to be the white one?"

"No, you could put the black one on top."

"Good."

"Then you move the dog under the paper—and the top one moves."

"Right . . . but you just told me that."

"Okay."

"So, that was it—one trick?"

"I suppose."

(Pause.)

"Fun."

Once we were old enough to sit away from our parents, age twelve to fourteen, the nine or ten boys close to the same age would gather in the last row. This was bad enough, but the sound system for the church's two microphones was located there in the middle of the row. We were not, under any circumstances, to touch anything. It was an old tube-style box, it got hot enough to melt crayons, and it became a game to tweak the knobs just enough to start the feedback process. Thinking back years later—knowing what happens to the sense of hearing as we age—the kids were probably the only ones able to detect the high-pitched squeal.

And when you had a week of "special meetings" with a visiting preacher, sitting in the first two pews because you got there late—these tedious diatribes—I mean sermons— were real desert experiences. Visions of tall glasses of water, Kool-Aid, and root beer marred the impact the preacher hoped to have on us, whatever that might have been—something we were doing wrong, I'm sure.

We were pretty sure there was a water fountain built into the pulpit; we just knew it.

We often knelt to pray, backwards with our arms resting on the pew, heads bowed. Occasionally we would draw on the soles of the shoes behind us.

"Elmer, what is on the bottom of your shoe?"

"It seems to be a picture of a dog, or maybe a rodent."

"We were sitting behind the Swartzes."

"Ah, those boys . . ."

"Must have been Tim. He's the artist."

"Right, Teddy can't draw."

Tim and I would wait for the "amen," pop up, and spin around to catch a glimpse of a sea of heads just visible above the backs of the pews, like sea turtles bobbing in the ocean, heading to the beach.

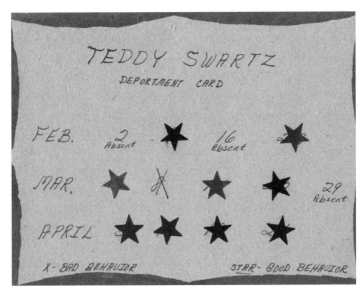

Sunday school memories are dominated by the gang of boys clustered into three grades, perhaps learning the stories of the Bible, perhaps not. My Mom sent this to me a number of years ago. I'm not sure what happened on March eighth, but I earned no star that day.

ϙ ϙ ϙ

Footwashing is a ritual practiced by Mennos to commemorate Jesus washing his disciples' feet during the Last Supper. In our Mennonite tradition, footwashing was held in the same esteem as communion, reflecting the servant nature of the followers of Jesus.

During footwashing we boys would crouch down and peer underneath the pews, watching men taking off their shoes and socks in preparation. Men's feet are ugly: corns, bent toes, and toenails that start to disappear as they age. The feet were very white; if it was summer, it was shocking. Ours were brown by the first week of June. Only men's feet were visible to us, because the women had a private room in the back. It would not do at all for a woman's bare feet to be seen in church—especially knowing that stockings had just come off of those feet.

Communion was held during the same service. For many years communion was not a grace-filled moment of coming to the Lord's table, but rather a reward for being right with the body of Christ and with the bishop—I mean with God. Preparatory meetings were called to see if you were penitent enough to receive communion. I guess that's why we only had it twice a year. It must have been exhausting for God—I mean the bishop—to make sure all had "fixed their wrongs." People even fixed the wrongs they didn't know were wrongs until God—er, the bishop—pointed them out.

Communion was a solemn event. Either someone had baked very small loaves of bread, or cut a large loaf into neat squares, which were broken and passed to each row. Not to the kids—you had to be a member to participate in the ritual. For us, watching this event meant wondering what we would choose if we could pick the communion food: cinnamon rolls, pumpkin pie, Nana's peanut butter cookies . . .

Then the passing of The Cup: a tall metal purple cup that looked like an ancient artifact, like the Holy Grail. We lusted after the grape juice (our church did not serve wine). The idea of the common cup made us squeamish. The deacon—an unsmiling, stern man we were very sure hated kids—would wipe the edge of the cup after each participant drank. Took those germs right off.

We were glad we didn't have to drink after William, who wasn't right in the head. We'd heard rumors that it was a failed attempt at courting that pushed him over the edge. The idea of William as a spurned lover intrigued us. He was cared for by his two single sisters. It was William who, at the quietest moments in church, would rise up on one hip and let loose with a trumpeting release of gas.

Studies have shown that flatulence is the only act that makes people of all cultures laugh. It is the supreme equalizer. William became a heroic figure to the group of adolescent boys. He didn't care, and he didn't try to hide it! And such eloquence! It seemed he could pass gas in couplets. Perhaps William was unaware of us kids in general; however, he knew his audience. He would, after one of his particularly fine "comments" on the service to that point, begin a slow turn to look over his shoulder and peer at us, who were desperately trying not to laugh—which would incur the wrath of the deacon. When William knew we heard him—heck, they might have heard him in Philadelphia—a slow sly smile would creep across his face as if to say, "Eh? Pretty good one. I'll bet you wish you had such powers."

Tim's comment years later: "Not only were we sitting in our pew, but now his as well."

William reached legendary status the morning he sneezed and his false teeth flew out, skidding up several rows. Also achieving heroic status was Jim, who calmly picked up the teeth and handed them back to William, who tucked them in his pocket. Now the image of his teeth, wrapped in a handkerchief in the right pocket of his plain coat, was stuck in our heads the rest of the morning. Would he bother to wash them before putting them back in?

Athletics and imagination: baseball, *The Sound of Music*, and dance

A crucial building block of acting is the understanding of body: how it moves, what it communicates, how it leads us to emotional connections. It's part of the reason why dance, a first cousin to theater, can be a great discipline to further theater education.

Dance, however, was not part of my education as a child. It was suspect as a tool of the world and its right-hand man, the devil. Should we concentrate too much on that weak vessel, the body, it's not far then to the slippery slope of sexuality and the many pitfalls waiting there amid the sweat and touching.

So no dancing. How then does a Mennonite youth discover the limits and possibilities of the human body?

Well, there was baseball. Baseball has always been there. I followed my leader Tim to baseball, and it was and remains a powerful tether between us.

We were nuts about it, inventing variations of the game inside the house and outside. Inside baseball was played in the living room, on the floor. We'd divide the stack of baseball cards up and thus draft our teams; then defensively lay out our cards in their positions. Home plate was by the front door, left-field wall was the marble-top table, bat and ball were a pencil and a ping pong ball.

The pitcher rolled the ball from center field position. A ball caught in the air was an out; there were strikeouts, and when a ground ball rolled over a card, the batter was out. As you can imagine, the range of those players lying there staring upward toward the ceiling was limited.

The right-field wall was inviting—it was a short porch, like the old Polo Grounds or Yankee Stadium—but you had to get some lift for a home run: up and into the stereo system.

The stereo system. Yes, though dancing was forbidden, we did have music; mostly gospel, some children's albums, and a strange addition: Barry Sandler's *Ballads of the Green Berets*. Ordinarily this was not an album my parents would have purchased. They had thought they had purchased the soundtrack for *The Sound of Music.*[11] But there must have been a mistake in the shipping department, for instead of the hills being alive with music, the disc in the sleeve was *Ballads of the Green Berets.* This was before the Vietnam War became unpopular in the U.S., and it still seemed heroic to send young men to kill and die on the other side of the world.

> Fighting soldiers from the sky
> Fearless men who jump and die
> Men who mean just what they say
> The brave men of the Green Beret
> Silver wings upon their chest
> These are men, America's best. . . .

To our folks' chagrin, we learned all the words to the "Ballad."

We also played Little League. Tim played at first, but I didn't play as soon as I was old enough. My recollection is that I was too shy, but Tim told me recently, "I wanted to play for Mr. Dawson, coach of the Pirates, and he was reluctant to draft families (brothers always played on the same team), so I discouraged you from playing." *Really?*

And I thought he was looking out for me.

He wasn't drafted by the Pirates, but rather the A's—and while warming him up before a game the coach of the A's minor league team asked me, "Why aren't you playing?"

(A shrug.)

To Tim: "Why isn't he playing?"

(Another shrug. We were a talkative couple of kids.)

"Give this kid a shirt."

I got a shirt. My organized baseball career had begun. The next year I was ten, which meant I had the option of moving up to

---

11 For thousands of Mennonites across North America, *The Sound of Music* was the first movie they saw in a theater. It was a combination of the wholesomeness of the movie and perhaps the rebellion of the 1960s. It wasn't as if the entire Mennonite church across the U.S. and Canada said, "Hey, maybe we won't all go collectively to hell if we watch a movie—in a theater—in color," but it was close. Yes, the door was now open, the slippery slope was erected.

the big field, the "majors." But I was held back in order to pitch. I suppose they saw potential and started me in the second game of the season. There was no real instruction at that level, so having watched Tim pitch for years (being his personal catcher for hours at home), I went out to the mound with a general idea of how my body should move.

I had also seen many pictures—Juan Marichal, Sandy Koufax, Whitey Ford, Bob Gibson—and knew there was a style to it. Style seemed to be important. In the third inning, I was struggling with control. The coach, Mr. Moore, came out, took the ball, and brusquely said, "This isn't ballet." A little too much style apparently.

I was crushed, and never attempted to pitch in organized baseball again. But I have been intrigued over the years by dance. Before I get too old I'd like to incorporate those two—ballet and baseball . . .

> The routine starts with classical music. An actor walks out onstage and takes a pitcher's stance, receives the signal from the catcher, and mimes a pitch. He moves through a series of at-bats, registering the elation and despair inherent in these encounters. At some point a woman dancer comes out and stands beside him and begins an unrelated but vaguely reminiscent dance routine. As the music advances the two motions begin to morph into each other, until the woman is now "pitching" and the pitcher is now dancing. She scratches, spits, and reacts to the calls of the umpire. He is lost in the movements of the dance.

Before I retire I do want to do that. If I could find Mr. Moore alive, I would bring him to the show and say, "It can be, after all, ballet."

After the "ballet disaster" I was moved up to the majors, where I served my time as a "two-inning player." Everyone had to play two innings per game, and when you are the youngest, that was often all the playing time you were afforded. I got one hit that year, a line single over second base off of Larry Wilkins, a lefty from my class in elementary school. Three years later at age thirteen, again serving time as a sub at the next level of play, when the field size expanded, I got one hit all year, a line single over second base off of . . . yes: Larry Wilkins.

I owned Larry Wilkins.

The league bought new uniforms after my last year, so I kept mine. It hung in my closet for years, and when the boys were little, it became a favorite Halloween costume.

In our yard, home plate was a piece of sandstone, a flagstone roughly one inch think, somewhat in the shape of a home plate, which is why it ended up in the yard—as home plate. (Not "home base" like Nana said, but home plate. Home was a plate, the others were bases.[12])

Nana never quite got the whole sports infatuation and didn't have the heart of a competitive athlete. Once, while watching a ball game on TV with us, Nana asked, "Why does he pitch it so the other fella can't hit it? That doesn't seem fair." That was Nana, concerned not about the competitive spirit of the game but instead with the fairness of the situation and whether grace was extended.

In the summer our home plate absorbed the heat from the sun. Because we played in bare feet all summer, you didn't want to stand too long on home plate, and when you slid home you risked catching your foot or toe or knee on the edge of the stone.

We played a lot of three-man baseball: Tim, me, and usually the neighbor, Tim Greenland, who lived two houses down. Tim G. was born in central Pennsylvania and was the first person we ever heard use the term *you'ins*, which run together became *y'ins*—not to be confused with *you all*, run together as *y'all*.

One hot afternoon, Tim G. announced that the day before, he had become so angry with his father, Ray—always dressed in green

---

12 Look, these distinctions are important: it's a catcher's mitt, but everything else is a glove. Perhaps in years past they were all known as mitts, but as the glove evolved into its modern form with distinctive fingers, the term mitt (as in mitten—no fingers) remained with the catcher's mitt, not glove. Are we all clear on this important and even crucial distinction? More on this later, when we will discuss skits, bits, and sketches. Class is now dismissed.

coveralls and wielding a cigarette—that he cursed at him. I asked what he said, thinking he *might* have said *shit*.

"I called him a g**d***motherf******sonofab****."

I was speechless—pretty sure that was the first time I'd heard any of those words in isolation, let alone strung together in a rhythmic chant like that. The words, like pollen, hung in the air, until . . .

" . . . Okay . . . who's up?"

One day we went out to play and discovered home plate was gone. It didn't need to be moved to mow the yard, so that couldn't be why it was missing—who would steal a stone? We played without it, the patch of dead grass substituting for home. It remained a puzzle until we got into the car for church that Sunday, and there, covering the rusty hole in the floorboard of our black Ford, was home plate.

What?? That was the best we could do? The best in automotive repair? Our home plate? Wow. Okay.

Elementary School: Isolation, Commonality, and a Moment of Triumph in a Dog Food Bag[13]

THEATER AND ACTING often mark an intersection of vulnerability and confidence, strength and sensitivity, courage and anxiety. That sounds a bit like elementary school.

Second grade—the year I received my first pair of glasses. If you've never worn glasses, it's a bigger deal than you might think, for a six year old. Your relief at being able to see more clearly is tempered by a responsibility for which you are not ready.

The first thing in the morning is to put them on: a simple task which involved seemingly hours of frustration looking for them, but the catch is, you can't see well enough to look for them. Did they fall behind the bed this time, or under the bed? Did you leave them in the bathroom?

Playing sandlot football with glasses meant that the bridge of your nose was in constant scab mode. You had to play with them; you couldn't see well enough without them. And yes, there was always tape on the corners.

Second grade was also the year I discovered a whole room full

---

13 Purina.

of books at school—the library. My first book was beneath my reading level, but it caught my attention. It was the story of a boy who became a hero by defeating a giant. The climax came when he disguised a bird as a stone and threw the "stone" higher than the giant, winning the contest and saving the town. I have never since been without a book. Books became part of my costumes, as normal as pants. A good friend of mine will always ask as part of a normal conversation, "So, what are you reading?"

Mrs. Elliott was a teacher who was always color-coordinated, wore lots of makeup, and lots of perfume. Her purse matched her shoes, her shoes matched her earrings, her earrings matched her glasses, which she wore on a chain around her neck.

I was punished twice in seven years of elementary school, both times unjustly. One of them was when Mrs. Elliott was reading us a book in which the hero won the day by fooling the bad guys into thinking the red part of his clothing was fire. Okay, so it wasn't an especially deep book. That day I was wearing argyle socks with red in the pattern, and so I "scared" the boy across the aisle by raising my foot toward him, displaying that dangerous red. He played along and acted like he was afraid. I had obviously been taken by the story.

Suddenly in the middle of this imaginative ingestion of the story I felt myself grabbed from behind, arms pinned against my sides, and shaken. This was an acceptable form of punishment in 1962, to be shaken.

Mrs. Elliott said, "There *will* be no kicking in my class."

The injustice still sits with me almost fifty years later. I was too stunned to speak, to defend myself. The words I wanted to say died in my mouth.

"I was only acting out the story."

In second grade we also got a new student; his name was Peter. He had glasses, like me, and he seemed a little out of place, just like me. But he spoke with an accent, one that I had not heard before.

The *R*s were different; certain words came out wrong.

He spoke with a strong German accent. Not Pennsylvania Dutch, which is a low German dialect spoken by some of my relatives; this was a native German speaker learning a second language.

Peter and I became friends. One day I visited his house, where we played with army figures and tanks—and he had a lot of tanks. In our house we weren't supposed to play with army figures, but they were always an attraction for us. It took me a while to figure out what was different about Peter's set of army figures.

I realized after a time what it was that was different. All of his figures were gray, not green. Green was the color of the Allied forces in World War II; gray was for the German armies.

It was less than twenty years since the end of World War II, and army figures sold at that time were still patterned after the icons of World War II—not Vietnam, not Korea, but the big one—World War II. Peter's figures were gray: the German Army. Why? His dad had driven a tank in World War II.

So there we were: the Mennonite boy and the German boy, playing army under the maple trees in eastern Pennsylvania, United States, where, since it was Peter's set, the victors wore gray.

❦ ❦ ❦

Since becoming involved in theater, I've realized how much I love costumes. Many times the addition of a hat, a cape, a pair of glasses can help an actor "find the character," affecting posture, voice, and carriage. Makes me wish I could have been more creative during Halloween as a kid.

Halloween was not something good Mennos in that period participated in. But our school had a Halloween parade each year, where you would dress up and walk around the school. For some reason, we were allowed to take part in this. The cool guys would often wear their football uniforms, but there were also ghosts, witches, and superheroes. However, organized football was out, and my folks weren't going to waste money on a store-bought costume. Instead, Mom found a cheap mask of a dog, then cut holes in a twenty-five-pound Purina dog food bag for my head and arms.

That's what I wore at the big Halloween parade, a dog food bag. I also had to wear my glasses overtop the mask, taping them on so they wouldn't fall off. With my eyesight at 20/200, I couldn't possibly march around the school in a dog food bag without them.

Principal Hess did single me out for a comment: "Love the glasses; nice touch."

Yay, Mom!

I think three dogs followed me home that day.

Christmas tree

Christmas at our house did not include a tree. Once again the church loomed over us—so no tree. No Santa sightings, no elves, nothing to confuse the children as to why we had the holiday, and—no tree.

What was so bad about a tree? It must have been a little too festive, all that glitter and frivolity, drawing us away from the true meaning of Christmas: commerce . . . I mean, Jesus. Instead, we had a cardboard fireplace reassembled every year and festooned with fake snow, and stockings thumbtacked onto the front. Now a fireplace—wasn't that a subtle leaning toward the traditions of jolly St. Nick sliding down the chimney to fill the stockings hung there? *Hmmm.* Made for interesting conversations at school:

"So, when are you getting your tree?"

"Ah . . . we don't get a tree."

"Really?"

"No, we . . . put up a fireplace."

"What?"

"We put together a fireplace."

"A real fireplace, with bricks and stuff?"

"No, it's cardboard . . . then we hang our stockings off the cardboard fireplace."

(Pause.)

"That's weird."

"I know."

"We have a tree *and* a real fireplace."

Right, and I'll bet you get fireworks on the Fourth of July, too.

It *was* good-quality cardboard; packed away after New Year's, then put together next year. And the stockings had white trim with the names spelled out in glitter: Timmy, Teddy, and Tina. It takes a pretty healthy thumbtack to keep a stocking properly affixed to a cardboard fireplace. When it was finally Christmas morning and time to look in our stockings, they were no longer on the fireplace. Physics would have dictated that the weight of the filled stockings would've by now pulled the fireplace over. While Mom found it hard to be warm, or to be effusive with praise, or to tell us that she was proud of us, her Christmas stockings were legendary. It was one of the things she did better than anybody we knew. She spent all year, it seems, finding those cool little things that delighted us each Christmas morning.

When Tim was in fourth grade, right before Christmas vacation, his teacher asked, "Does anyone *not* have a tree at home?"

Tim raised his hand.

"Would you like to take the class tree home?"

"Would I? *Would I*?!"

So Tim, a skinny kid with a buzz cut and thick plastic-rimmed glasses, dressed in a used coat purchased at the Hodge Podge (a secondhand store in Phoenixville), dragged a Christmas tree the half mile from school to our house, where, to my parents' credit, they put it up—probably draped with leftover fake snow. Until the day Uncle Norman came for a pastoral visit and they put it on the back porch. He was still visiting when Tim came home and hollered, "Hey, where's the Christmas tree?"

SCENE 3

Calling and Clowning

IN THE EARLY 1960s we discovered a green metal box in our house that spoke of an ancient time, perhaps as long ago as thirteen years previous. It contained money, coins, and bills with strange faces and languages imprinted on them and many, many black and white snapshots. Among them this one, below.

At age twenty-one Dad spent a year in Germany, rebuilding communities after the war. It was the first wave of a newly formed

That's Dad on the right, in 1951, in PAX.

service program—the PAX program.[14] That year was his greatest life-changing experience; it informed his view of the world and his views on theology, nationalism, and the importance of the peace position the Mennonites have held. The role of the church's compliance in the rise of Nazism persuaded him that "if it could happen there, it could happen here." It was from this position that he and Mom instilled in us a healthy distrust of nationalism and a belief in the separation of church and state—not just to protect the state, but the church as well.

All of us learned to appreciate this viewpoint and all it taught us, but when we were small, it was the photo that *inspired* us. The composition of the snapshot is remarkable, and the joy of young men clowning is enchanting. We were delighted that our Dad would make people laugh. When this photo showed up many years later in a video presentation about PAX, the narrator noted Dad's name and said, "Now we know where Ted received his inspiration and genetic capabilities for comedy."

Espelkamp was the place Dad lived during his life-changing year. It affected him, his married life, and his relationships with his parents and his children. It was a sacred place, but he made people laugh, also a sacred place. Dad didn't want to be known as a clown; it was important to him that communities understood he was more than this. I know what he means but I also don't ever want to diminish the value of simply making people laugh.

In 2006, Sue and I traveled to Germany to visit our youngest son Derek and see those areas we grew up hearing about. We made contact with a couple still living in Espelkamp, in the same development where Dad had worked. They met us at a park and led us onto their street. This was the town that lived in our minds from Dad's stories and the black and white Polaroid snapshot. I suppose I was expecting the block buildings and mud. But when we turned the corner I was stunned by the beauty, the riot of colors of flowers in full bloom. We slept for

---

14 PAX is Latin for peace. The young men, while in Germany, were known by the locals as the "Paxboys." For more information visit www.paxmcc.com.

Espelkamp in 1951 and in 2006.

three nights in the house that Dad helped build in 1951.

Because all three of the kids in the family have a strong artistic bent, we get asked sometimes where it came from. There wasn't visibly a lot of influence. However, Mom was a huge music aficionado and she exposed us to concerts and choral programs.

SCENE 4

A Sad Tale of Unrequited Love as Understood in the Eighth Grade Sense

I THOUGHT MICHELLE KRAWLY was the most beautiful creature on this earth. Blond hair slightly tousled, soft smooth skin . . . or so I imagined.

I admired her from afar, way afar. See, she was a Krawly and sat in the third row. I, being a Swartz, sat in the last row, right behind Mike Stranick and Bill Stribula and across from Bill McAfee, Kay Pastalak, and Harvey Numaricktor.

It was right before Social Studies, Mr. Strange's class (and let me tell you, he was).

I had on a new shirt that day, one I really liked. It was a pullover, dark blue, made out of that fake silk kind of material. I really liked how it felt. It was the kind of shirt that highlighted muscle tone—if I had any at the time.

Just as I reached the doorway to enter, there she was: Michelle Krawly.

I don't know what motivated her to leave her seat and reach that doorway the exact time in history as I did.

Fate?

Karma?

A shifting of the moons?

Did she just . . . forget her pencil?

There was a tightening in my chest, and I know I breathed just a little faster. I moved to the side to let her pass, and then . . . she smiled at me.

Now that would have been enough. I could hear birds sing from that smile.

But that wasn't all. She opened her mouth and actually spoke to me. She did!

She said, "I like your shirt."

She liked my shirt.

Not just "excuse me," which would have been enough. Not just "hi," which would have been more than enough.

No no, this was more, much more. This was a statement of affirmation in direct response to something I was wearing.

My opinion of my mother's taste in clothing had risen 100 percent.

Well, I needed to respond. This was what I had dreamed would happen. I spoke the first words that came into my head.

"So do I."

So do I?

The first *and* last words I ever spoke to Michelle Krawly.

SCENE 5

Love, Acne, and the Art of Being Funny

IN NINTH GRADE I followed Tim to Christopher Dock Mennonite High School in Lansdale, Pennsylvania, where the classes were small and the people were friendly—it was actually possible to know everyone in your class.

It was here that I started creating a reputation as a funny person—never the class clown, which would be too much attention. But rather someone who was always looking for what made a situation funny—it was a way to make people like me, the role humor has played for millions of people before me. Humor: the lubricant between people, the access point for commonality—many of us learn this intuitively, as a survival technique.[15]

---

15 Humor was a huge part of our lives as kids. Lee and I used to say we had a collective eighty years of comedic historical study. Tim was my first partner in the study of what was funny, how and why it was funny. I owe a great debt to those who have gone before. Comedy is built on the work of preceding generations . . . for me the Jewish sense of comedy was invaluable—from the Marx brothers to Jerry Lewis, to Woody Allen, Mel Brooks, Andy Kauffman, to Robert Klein, to Jerry Seinfeld, to Lewis Black and Jon Stewart, I learned inflection, beats and timing. Then there was Monty Python. Tim introduced me to Monty P. albums, then the TV show was picked up by PBS. What made Python brilliant became a template for Lee and me—intelligent plus silly, with complete commitment to the moment.

Between tenth and eleventh grade, my classmate Alan reported to me that we had two new girls coming the next fall—good-looking girls. We, the guys, were curious on the first day, scouting the hallways and classrooms. I saw a self-assured girl with straight hair parted in the middle, an adorable beauty mark on her upper lip, who filled out her dress in a wonderful way. She was smart, cute, earthy, strong, opinionated, and . . . dating an older guy, Mike.

So, Sue Althouse was safe to become friends with. We hung out at basketball games and during lunch; we made each other laugh. That summer she asked me to be coeditor of the yearbook, claiming afterwards no ulterior motives. It was an excruciating fall, spending so much time together, wondering just what to do with this growing joy and pain emanating from my chest.

I kept the gum wrappers she used, her old school IDs, the movie stubs . . . A little pitiful, I know. I had never gone on an actual date, and I didn't know how that particular tradition was supposed to unfold. We just spent a lot of time together . . . a *lot* of time together. A gang of us went to a birthday party for the sister of the guy Sue was dating—and some of my friends asked me if they should take him, the guy, outside and take care of the issue. So it was that obvious, was it? *No thanks guys, I'll just suffer in silent agony over here.* The first time you fall in love, even at age sixteen, is never quite replicated.

I recently rediscovered a Bible of Sue's. I had grabbed it off the shelf to use in a photo shoot. I flipped open the front cover and found this:

Sue, I give you this Bible along with my love. And I hope you will cherish this gift more than any other I give to you. You can get along without me, but you can't get along without God. So if we ever come to a fork in the road of life and you go one way and I go another, remember, this book will help you through the hardest times. —Mike[16]

That fork in the road came to be December 6, 1973, the best day of my life to that point. Sue and I officially started dating, following a hayride. Menno youth didn't dance, but we did have hayrides. Her dad drove her to the ride, I took her home. On that drive, after a party, where I was perfecting my passive-aggressive skills of sullen silence in response to a perceived hurt, Sue, at the stop sign at the end of Hilltown Road, leaned over and put the car in park—in order to talk.

I missed that signal, and when she leaned over, we kissed for the first time.

So that was what heaven felt like.

I do remember thinking: *Where do the noses go?* And: *I sure wish I didn't have glasses on.* Every trip to Doylestown thereafter, to this point, we stop and kiss—eliciting, when they were small, groans and noises of general grossness from the boys.

---

16 Assumed name.

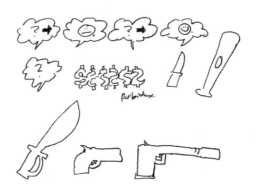

SCENE 6

Knives, Blood, Beer, Cigarettes, and Hair

AT FIFTEEN YEARS old, I started cutting meat after school and on Saturdays. I worked at the small market my folks owned, wrestling with the sides of beef, front and hindquarters, weighing between 150 and 200 pounds. By age seventeen, I was striving to prove myself, having the strength to wrestle the quarters while people (sometimes young women) watched. It was theater of a sort—the blood contributing to the drama of the moment. It meant not forgetting the tool at hand was sharp enough to take my own leg or finger off, should I slip. It meant testosterone, a whiff

of danger, a script, but with possibilities of mistakes. Yes, it was theater.

In early August 1976 I was manning the meat department on a Thursday night. Carol E. was a steady customer most Thursday nights and she was notorious for coming in fifteen minutes before we closed. You couldn't complete the cleanup too soon, because Carol might come blowing in the door, hollering out her greetings as she stormed down the aisle.

On this occasion she ordered a rump roast, which needed to be carved out of the round. If you look at a steer from the side, this would be found close to the rear hip, before the back leg begins to taper down. The less active the muscles of the steer are, the more tender the cut. The reason the filet mignon is the most tender is a result of where it lies: the muscle that runs up the inside of the backbone, making it almost exclusively non-weight bearing.

The rump roast was a tender cut but also required the most excavation. A round weighs about eighty to ninety pounds, and the rump would take about ten minutes to have ready for her. A number of cuts in meat cutting are done with the knife in the forward position—imagine holding a pencil. The finer cuts are with the knife in this position. If you need more strength for the cut, you hold the knife backhand—imagine fisting the handle in much the way Anthony Perkins did in *Psycho*.

This night, the block was a bit slippery with blood. As I pulled the round around for the backhand cut, it began to slip off the butcher block and I quickly thrust my right arm underneath to catch it, the same arm gripping backhand the ten-inch boning knife. I caught it, but the eighty pounds of beef drove the knife into my thigh. Carol at the counter was watching and she saw the look on my face.

"Did you just stab yourself?"

Me, frozen in place, still holding the round: "Yeah."

"Oh my."

"I'm not sure what to do."

"I'm married and a mother; you can take your pants off."

If she wasn't married I wonder if I would have been allowed to take my pants off—or maybe she just wouldn't have been so attentive. I stripped my pants off, wrapped the towel around my bleeding leg, put on two aprons—one which came to my knees around the front of me, the other covering my back—and off we went to the hospital—me and Sue, who was working the cash register that night.

I guess Carol never got her roast.

Beer and cigarettes

I'm not exactly sure why not smoking or drinking became such an ironclad dictum for me. Maybe because I knew I might be a candidate for abuse? In any event in my late teens, it became an identity—I was the guy who was pretty cool and funny without the need to drink. It had become a point of what . . . stubbornness? a point of honor? an "I-can-be-just-as-cool-as-you-without-smoking-or-drinking" stance?

On a couple of occasions I acted as designated driver. There was one memorable night with Rodney and Dale when they had secured a case of beer and between them drank the entire case of warm brew, while at a drive-in movie watching two truly horrific films that can only be filed under "this is for young men hoping to get a couple of boob shots."

Having now acquired a taste for a good microbrew beer I can only imagine the experience of twelve room-temperature Millers; it's not surprising that when I stepped out of the car that night I put my foot into Dale's deposited rejection of his share of that fine vintage. At least he could have warned me.

A friend from church went, not to a Mennonite college, but rather to big scary Penn State University. On his fall break, he told me at church he wanted to introduce me to pot.

I laughed at him.

Found out later he didn't like being laughed at; we didn't talk again until our twenty-year high school reunion. By then we had forgiven each other. I should have asked him if he brought "the stuff." That would have been great—wait twenty years for a punch line.

While in college with kids mostly twelve to thirteen years younger, one student grilled me:

"I'd like to sit down sometime and talk to you about your drug experience."

"My what?"

"You know, your drug period."

"Drug period—as in the use of?"

"Yeah."

He seemed eager for details of debauchery and decadence, culminating perhaps in a heroic rescue by God and true love.

"Who said I had a drug period?"

"I just assumed . . . you know . . . you're in theater, politically radical, funny—I've seen pictures of the hair length . . . "

"Geez, thanks for that . . . affirmation? But I don't have a drug period."

"Oh."

He seemed disappointed. Sorry.

Though I have never smoked, I have used cigarettes many times on stage—even written them into character development. In the play *Glimmer, Glimmer and Shine* in 2004 I played a foul-mouthed, chain-smoking heroin addict with a heart of gold. At one point in rehearsal, during the pot smoking scene, the director said to my young coactor, pointing to me, "Jason, I know he's never smoked pot, and I know you have, so why does *he* look like the only who knows what he's doing?"

Reminds me of an old axiom for acting: there are three reasons why you know how to do something on stage—you've done it yourself, you've seen someone else do it, or you make it up.

What's with the hair?

If you didn't grow up in the 1960s and '70s it's hard to communicate what a big deal hair was for guys. During the early '70s to grow your hair long was an outward symbol of rebellion, an attempt at

counterculture. It started in the '60s of course, but it took until the '70s to really catch on in suburban America. We weren't always sure what it was we were rebelling against, but it was something: the Vietnam War was still raging, Richard Nixon was becoming a symbol of what was wrong with politics in America, or perhaps you just needed to be or do something different from your parents.

If you grow your hair long today it can be just fine; you could shave your head the next day and that would be accepted too. But in the '70s long hair hadn't been seen in culture since perhaps Thomas Jefferson's neat little ponytail, so it was a sign of greater rebellion.

At about fifteen I started fighting with my parents about hair. It seems ludicrous now that this was our battleground; if you had to pick something, hair was a pretty innocuous argument. My parents must have been afraid of the urge to grow long hair because they felt it would be followed immediately by a slide down the slippery slope of cigarettes, beer, hard liquor, rampant sex, and marijuana use. I didn't want anyone to tell me how long my hair should or could be. I consented to haircuts in August of 1973 right before senior picture, and I got my next haircut in May right before graduation. That May I remember thinking, *Now that I've graduated no one will ever tell me to get my hair cut again. In fact, I may* never *get it cut again.*

Ⓧ I REALLY LIKE THIS ONE!

Marriage and Failure

WHEN EACH OF our boys passed the age of nineteen still unmarried, I had a private celebration. I was nineteen when Sue and I got married. I realized just how young we were, and was happy that they wouldn't be marrying that young.

Our wedding was nontraditional for that time in the Mennonite church. It was outside, on our high school lawn. We were dressed semicasually—Sue in a dress her sister had made for twenty-five dollars—and the guys in flared pants and rented ruffled shirts.

Sue's and my wedding, 1974.

When asked the secret of marrying young we often say, "naive persistence." One of the things about marrying young in the era in which we did was our naiveté. Marriage was going to work; it never entered our minds that it wouldn't. When this is the basis in which you enter in, it can help get you through the inevitable bumps along the way.

However, because we started so young, we grew up together, and it always felt as if Sue had a head start because of her maturity. I looked to her to make important decisions, she handled the money and the schedule. I handled . . . let's see . . . what was I handling? Those first years of marriage included cutting meat for Dad and Mom, lots of fast pitch softball, lots of basketball . . . what else? Who was I?

During our first year, at our high school reunion, when we were "reporting in," I said, "I'm working for my dad, which is where I'll be until he sells me the business." It seemed like the natural response; I didn't see any potential beyond that. Why did that upset Sue so much?

After three years of marriage we were ready for a change. Well, Sue was ready for a change—either to church-related service or back to college to finish her degree. Finishing the degree seemed the best option, so we packed our meager possessions and moved back to Virginia—where Sue finished her elementary education degree.

Two years later, upon our return to Pennsylvania, Sue was offered a job at Penn View Christian School. I decided, after having lived in a college town without attending, that maybe I was ready for college. What timing, what forethought! Montgomery Community College was cheap and accessible and I had a great time—feeling old at twenty-five and experienced with writing papers without computer or typewriter. When I handed in a history paper, the teacher looked at my twenty hand-printed pages, and asked, "What—were you a monk in a previous life?"

He was also the teacher who called me Jed for four weeks before I corrected him—apparently my creative form of writing Ted had a little too much loop in the T.

That year, the phys. ed. teacher told me that she had dreamed of me in front of hundreds of people, and wondered what that might mean. I didn't know. It didn't make a lot of sense then to think about cutting meat in front of hundreds of people.

❡ ❡ ❡

The small supermarket was struggling; it seems we had made the brilliant decision, four years earlier, to move from a small meat market to a full-service supermarket, investing in a retail model that was quickly growing extinct. Just at the time grocery stores were becoming behemoths or downsizing into specialty shops, there we were, still running a small supermarket, going in the wrong direction, like salmon leaping upstream. Rather like investing your life savings in the telegraph business right about the time the telephone was invented.

Recently Dad told me, "I knew it wasn't going to work after the first week." Wow, four years of anticipated dread and loss. All their hopes, dreams, aspirations set to begin spinning on a treadmill to nowhere.

The controller for the Association of Independent Groceries, who had money in the game, told us, "I have been on the fast track to success, and my advice is: Don't compromise your principles." Mom and Dad didn't compromise principles—they didn't sell cigarettes, they treated customers respectfully, offered quality at a fair price, never cheated the public—but it didn't help the business succeed either.

Does integrity ring hollow when the bills can't be paid? Swartz's Market is where I learned that sometimes, perhaps many times, just bending your back and working harder doesn't always mean financial success. It also informed a life-long paradoxical journey with the meaning of success. In our North American economic system, making money indicates success. To not compromise values in the face of financial ruin is not often regarded as success.

Art is especially hard to quantify as successful. Recently I performed in two shows in the Washington, D.C., area. Both shows were self-produced, always a risk monetarily. The other actor and I had fun, the shows were a rousing artistic success, the applause was long and sustained; people were engaged, entertained, moved, and given food for continued thought—and the company lost $1,000 and the lead actor (me) didn't get paid. So, a success? Depends on your definition of success—the standing ovation doesn't pay for health insurance or groceries.

When the store finally closed in 1986, it felt a bit like putting down the beloved, aged family pet—relief and pain at the same time. You grieve the loss but you're also glad Bucky's no longer crapping on the rug.

Now what?

Act 2

Rising Action

Wherein suspense builds, the basic conflict is complicated by the introduction of related secondary conflicts, including various obstacles that frustrate the protagonist's attempt to reach his goal.

Hearing a Call ...
But Which One?

AFTER OUR FAMILY'S store closed, I was adrift. The relief I felt at the removal of the pressure of a struggling business was replaced by uncertainty about job and career. And I continued to be frustrated with my place in life. I took a job painting houses, and Sue became pregnant with our third son.[17]

Coaching, the avocation I thought could become a vocation, was becoming impossible with three young boys. I moved from junior varsity basketball coach to varsity assistant—a chance to stay connected to the guys on the team and still work with Tim Ehst, good friend and head coach. High school basketball is a season that starts in late October and goes through the end of February, plus two weeks of camps in the summer. Road games can mean leaving at 3:30 in the afternoon and returning after eleven o'clock. There was a saying being passed around the coach's locker room: "Do you know why basketball coaches don't have affairs? No time."

Sue and I remained active as youth leaders at Plains Mennonite Church in Lansdale, for which coaching was a part of the train-

---

17 For a couple of intelligent adults, we hadn't yet figured out how this contraceptive thing worked. When asked at a wedding to give advice to the couple, I said, "Don't use foam." It perhaps looked as if we knew what we were doing—three boys, spaced out every two years, nice and orderly. But Ian, our middle son, was the only one we actually planned. Wouldn't have wanted it any other way now, of course.

ing. One of our responsibilities was to plan and carry out a church service. I must have mentioned to the group a play idea, because someone handed me a script book as a possible resource. It was a book of Isaac Air Freight sketches.

Isaac Air Freight is a forerunner of many who have worked in faith-based theater and comedy; their material was cutting edge for their time, and I was glad to have the book as a reference. As I read, I was surprised at how pedestrian I found the scripts and how much I disliked the theology. I thought, *I could write something better*. So I did: a one-act play, structured around a Sunday morning worship service. I believe I titled it "Because That's the Way We've Always Done It." It was a gently satirical view of the church from a youth's perspective—specifically the perception of a tradition-bound congregation teetering on the edge of irrelevance.

The church was enthusiastic about the service; in fact, it might have been this event that propelled church leaders to think of me as pastoral material. I had written a "tongue in cheek" sermon for a youth member to deliver, and it seemed to hit a chord for many congregants. Interesting that a comedy-infused "worship service" disguised as a play could be a part of a calling to be a pastor. Maybe we should have all just saved time and money and recognized the call to go directly into theater and comedy. Nah, that would have been too logical and organized for me.

In the winter of 1986, two couples from the congregation asked if I was interested in attending seminary to become a pastor. I would need to finish college first, having had the one year of community college before that first unplanned pregnancy interrupted my education.

Sue was game to go. She was the one who kept asking me, "What are your goals, what do you want?" I still wasn't sure, but I thought I could see myself in church leadership: I had a certain ability in front of people, and I thought perhaps I would be able to learn the skills to be an effective leader.

❦ ❦ ❦

My folks were sad to see the family move away, but there was a good chance we would return after five years in Virginia. Dad wanted one of his kids to be a preacher; to him it was the highest calling one could have. Just one more person I would disappoint by becoming an actor.

Leaving a community is never easy, but we felt ready for a change and, of course, expected to return. There was a going-away celebration at church, and I mentioned to a couple of guys my plans to leave something on the softball field. They spread the word, and instead of a small gathering of teammates, the entire thirty-five of us trouped out to the field where I ceremoniously doused my jock, socks, and batting gloves in gasoline and burned them at shortstop position. Yeah, it was corny, but it's the moment I remember from that evening. I never played shortstop on that field again.

When friends say, "Don't change," you know what they mean: don't forget us, don't become too good for us, don't let education take your faith from you, stay who you are. But most of us learn that simply growing older changes you, having kids changes you, an open mind changes you. Your basic personality may not change, but what you believe to be true should be challenged; a life of an open mind and heart guarantees that you will change.

The spring before we left for Eastern Mennonite College and Seminary in Virginia, actor Stephen Shenk performed at Plains Mennonite. It was an Easter service, and Steven performed his one-man show on the Passion of Christ. Just an actor and a plank of wood, a plank that became a table, a wall, a cross . . .

It made a huge impression on me. I never forgot the image of what could be done with something so simple. In later productions I would remember Stephen's austere acting and writing, and think: *What is absolutely necessary in this scene . . . and how clean can we make this turn*? I think the Last Supper scene in the Ted & Lee play *Fish-Eyes*, where the table is a simple plank laid across two barstools, is an homage to Stephen.

Adventures in education

I had found a house to rent several hundred yards from campus, just down the street, across from Eastern Mennonite High School. We cleaned and painted, Sue still nursing our youngest, while I registered for classes. The boys were four, two, and three months old, resilient at moving, the way children are. I was to begin an exciting new experience with new and interesting people; Sue was handling diapers, runny noses, and sick kids without the resources she had available at home—three sisters and parents, all within twenty minutes.

At thirty years old I was starting college again, horrible high school transcript in my pocket. I think my nickname from teachers must've been Ted "Is Capable of Doing Better" Swartz. I had a vague notion I made pretty good grades in elementary school, until my mother started sending elementary report cards to me a couple of years ago. (Why was she doing that?) I was four when I started kindergarten in 1961, and I guess I never really caught up. I had a growth spurt of six inches between tenth and eleventh grades. If I had waited another year to start school, gotten that spurt between ninth and tenth year, I might've even made the basketball team. But that would have put me a year behind Sue, admiring her from afar. Not a good trade-off.

Where was I? Starting college at thirty with three kids and a still somewhat vague notion of where I was headed.

I registered for an acting class, thinking it would be a good augmenting experience for someone headed to seminary—learning better diction, posture, comfort level in front of people. When I reached the registration table, the theater professor, Barbra Graber, informed me the class was full. Ah well, it was just a thought. Then she looked again at my name.

"Ted Swartz?"

"Yes."

"Tim's brother?"

"Yes."

"Okay—I'll make an exception."

And that exception changed my life. Barbra introduced me to a world I previously thought I might enjoy, yet I had no idea it would lead me to my place in the universe. Barbra was back that year from the University of Southern California, after getting her master's in fine arts in directing, with new interesting West Coast ideas about acting and theater.

She told me I had some natural ability but that I had a lot to learn. She was right. At that point, other than an occasional comedy sketch, I hadn't been onstage in thirteen years. My experience in plays was limited to one act in high school, where simply moving at the right time while remembering your lines was a great accomplishment.

Barbra's task was to lead a Mennonite community into a greater understanding and appreciation of theater and acting, and I was thrilled to be part of the effort. During one session on stage intimacy, the instructions were to touch your nose to your partner's face, neck, throat—in order to demystify the stage kiss. (We didn't have enough women, so I was paired with Darrell—that was also stretching.) Once you've led with your nose, it all seems a little silly and from there putting your lips together was just "more parts meeting." I like to think Darrell and I have maintained a special bond over the last twenty-five years.

Barbra's notes from my first acting scene with Sharon Gigley, in Shaw's *Arms and the Man*:

> Your timing is good. You find a rhythm for your communication, which works well comically. Your voice carries well and isn't held or pinched. I don't believe you need any voice work—though hearing you in a large auditorium would give me more cause to give you critique. Manner and voice are relaxed. Body is relaxed when you are speaking but still tenses up when not.

She asked if I was auditioning for the fall production of *A Midsummer Night's Dream*. However, Tom Baker, an old friend, had asked if I would coach junior varsity with him; I had said yes, thinking it would be fun to relate to kids and hang with Tom. What I hadn't expected was my inability to readjust to coaching, something I thought I had left behind. Also, I had not studied basketball since the last winter.

It was a valuable lesson. I felt I was playing catch-up all year; the boys got less of what I could have been—another striking example of my inability to be fully effective unless passionately committed. Basketball coaches are the ones in the restaurant drawing up plays and defensive schemes on napkins. I couldn't be that guy anymore; there was too much competing for space in my head.

The next option for auditioning was the spring production: *Quilters*, a wonderful show, but an all-woman cast. I would need to wait until the show of fall 1988—*The Foreigner*, by Larry Shue— to get on the main stage. I was cast as Froggy, a supporting role because of my relative inexperience, and I loved every minute of it.

The show called for a trapdoor, as a character sinks into the floor to great dramatic effect. Tech director Joe Hollinger had built a system under the stage with pulleys and counterweights, and in order for the trapdoor to be lowered, weight needed to be released. I volunteered to be the counterweight, riding the system underneath the stage. I also volunteered to perform the sound effects beneath the stage, breaking glass into a barrel, providing the sounds of general mayhem as a character, Ellard, stumbles around in the cellar. Actors should not be taking these roles between appearances on stage, but I was so enamored of the process of creating theater, I wanted to be in all possible roles.

The art of expressing anger

I have always been an avoider of conflict, sometimes to the detriment of honesty. It's perhaps a genetic thing for Mennonites in my family, and not very helpful for acting.

Acting class, scene work; I thought it was going well. Apparently not.

"Okay, stop."

"Yes?"

"Ted, aren't you supposed to be angry in the scene?"

"I suppose."

"'I suppose?'"

This response would be consistent with a favorite quote from *My Name Is Asher Lev* by Chaim Potok: "Ambiguity in art is like piss in coffee." So the response "I suppose" had no place in an acting class.

"Yes, I'm supposed to be angry."

"Why aren't you?"

"I am."

"No, I don't think you are."

"I am."

"Then why don't I think you are?"

"I don't know."

"That's apparent."

Okay—now I was getting angry.

"I should know if I'm angry."

"So you're angry now."

"Yes."

"Good. I still can't tell."

"Great."

"You nice Mennonite boys really don't know how to show anger."

"Boys? Really?"

Barbra had me take off my jacket and slam it on the ground while repeating the lines—harder and harder, the buckles sounding like shots when they hit the floor.

When I was finished, I was sweating and flushed, breathing heavily. Just like what happens when you . . . get angry.

Barbra either felt vindicated or smug; both were appropriate. Gosh, that felt good. Something had been unlocked. Now I was bellowing all the time; I knew how to be angry! Must've been a shock to the boys to witness this transformation:

"Great—Dad's hollering again."

"Is he mad?"

"I don't know."

"Could be he's just rehearsing something."

"On the safe side, let's just assume he's angry."

"Great."

Recently I was reminded of my "anger discovery stage." On Facebook you can post events, and then your friends can reply as to whether they are attending, unsure, or not attending. I was doing a show in Goshen, Indiana, so I posted an invitation on Facebook. Rich Troyer, who had been in *The Lion in Winter* with me when we were both college students in 1990, said he couldn't come, so I wrote him this message:

> Rich, I write a show I think you'll like—work for days, even weeks in the polishing of said show—make a decision to drive a long distance to bring the show to your town, buy new tires—rent a space—pay a choir—and you won't be there? Do I have that right?

Rich's answer:

> Ted, I'm picturing a scene from *The Lion in Winter* where you get really p***ed at your boys and throw all three of us to the ground and you pull yourself up to full height and then bellow in your loudest voice, "You try to d*** me. Well I d*** you back. God d*** you." I nearly peed myself the first time we ran that scene and I am nearly doing so now. I will reconsider, strongly reconsider. My wife and I can use a date night. Maybe we could do that. What show is it? Do you really think I will like it? Of course I will. I like everything you write. I can bring the kids too if that would make you happy, they usually enjoy, I mean they always love (that's what I meant to say) everything that you have ever written or ever will write or ever contemplate writing. You are the Milton to their Berle, the Cagney to their Lacey. You put the wit in witness, the bib on the Bible, the ugh in laughter. You are the great Oz and we will pay no attention to the man behind the curtain.

Anger became another tool in the toolbox, something shaped and honed to be available when a character needed it.

Highs and lows

During that first year back to college, determined to prove my scholarship after twelve years out in the work force, and following a profoundly underwhelming academic career in high school, I vowed to get an A—not merely in every class, but in everything I handed in: every quiz, every paper, every test. I actually enjoyed school; participated in class discussions, study groups. I became "one of those guys"—the ones in front of class with his hand up.

That vow for all As? I made it through the first year . . . until I started performing in plays. After that, family, rehearsals, and performances for six weeks, plus joining the pastoral team at church, made the vow a bit more difficult. However, I did manage to achieve one of those cum laude distinctions—not sure which one.

In the spring of 1990, my first year in seminary, I was cast in the lead role of *The Lion in Winter*, Henry II. I had directed a scene from *Lion* the year before, fell in love with the script, and lobbied Barbra to do this show at EMC. During auditions I made a crucial mistake: I tried to memorize the reading we were given, and I was overconfident about getting the role. I stumbled with the lines, did not acquit myself well at all. Barbra called me later and said it was not a given I would have this role. I learned my lesson, worked hard in callbacks, and have never taken for granted any audition since.

The play, a comedy/tragedy based on the real family of Henry II and Eleanor of Aquitaine, pushed me in ways I had never been pushed before. It was funny, dramatic, and wrenchingly painful. It was after this production I realized why I was here—I was to be an actor. The exhilaration I felt when onstage, communicating, connecting in ways never before felt, had a rightness, a sense of belonging. While I have since then felt fulfillment in teaching, writing, and directing in the field of theater, it is acting that remains at the core. Writing comes close occasionally, but the exhilaration of acting, perhaps because of the communal aspect, isn't quite matched.

As I was discovering this calling, Lee and I were performing here and there a couple of times a year, getting better as writers, expanding our repertoire of material. I was learning from him a better use of language and we further honed our symbiotic stage chemistry.

Laughter and the Bible: Comedic Exegesis Does Not Bring Fire down from Heaven

FIRST YEAR SEMINARY, Dorothy Jean Weaver's New Testament class. Dorothy Jean was our intense, bespectacled professor of New Testament and elementary Greek, deeply in love with the texts we studied. Our textbook was Jack Dean Kingsbury's *Matthew as Story*.

One afternoon Dorothy Jean told us, "This passage has classic themes with classic characters. Why don't you read this as a play with plot, characters, good guys, bad guys, conflict, and confrontation?"

I was at the back of the class memorizing lines and writing comedy sketches when she said this; it was like a dog smelling meat.

"Huhhh?"

She had caught my attention.

Despite my best intentions, I only seem to be effective as a writer, as an actor, as a person, when my passions are engaged, enflamed, and—dare I say it?—engorged. Okay, maybe not engorged, because while it doesn't *have* to sound a little dirty, it just *does*.

So, I was intrigued, interested . . . engorged.

Our text in class that day was from Matthew 16:5-12, where Jesus and the disciples are crossing Lake Galilee in a boat:

The disciples had forgotten to bring any bread when they crossed the lake. Jesus then warned them, "Watch out! Guard against the yeast of the Pharisees and Sadducees." The disciples talked this over and said to each other, "He must be saying this because we didn't bring along any bread."

Jesus knew what they were thinking and said:

"You surely don't have much faith! Why are you talking about not having any bread? Don't you understand? Have you forgotten about the five thousand people and all those baskets of leftovers from just five loaves of bread? And what about the four thousand people and all those baskets of leftovers from only seven loaves of bread? Don't you know by now that I am not talking to you about bread? Watch out for the yeast of the Pharisees and Sadducees!"

Finally, the disciples understood that Jesus wasn't talking about the yeast used to make bread, but about the teaching of the Pharisees and Sadducees (*Contemporary English Version*).

I found very funny the image of a confused group of disciples huddled together at one end of the boat—with Jesus at the other, waiting, perched serenely on the gunwale . . .[18]

He's thrown out yet another pithy, enigmatic saying: "Beware of the yeast of the Pharisees." I imagined this dialogue:

(Pause.)

"Yeast of the . . . what?!"

"Pharisees."

"Which Pharisees?"

"He didn't say—I think he means Pharisees in general."

"Why does he keep doing that?!"

---

18 Never mind the nautical impracticalities. I realize that professional fisherman, of which there were at least four, would never all pile into one end of the boat running the risk of swamping the boat, and dumping the Son of the Most High God into the Sea of Galilee. But one should never let facts get in the way of a good comedy image.

And it wasn't called a gunwale yet, I know, I know. 'Cause there weren't guns yet; again, don't let the facts get in the . . . okay.

"I don't know, look, you're the one who said we should follow him."

"I just liked the extra wine."

"What does he mean?"

"So . . . so, beware of the yeast of the Pharisees . . . yeast . . ."

"What about it?"

"You make bread with yeast, right?"

"Right, but not just yeast."

"What, beware of the baking powder of the Pharisees?"

"No, no . . . he's used the culinary motif before . . . it's the ingredients that are important, that's why the yeast."

"No, no, I think it's just the bread."

"The bread?"

"What about it?"

"Did you bring bread?"

"No, I thought you were going to bring the bread."

"Not me."

"We just left twelve baskets on the shore and you didn't bring any bread!"

Meanwhile Jesus is just sitting, watching, waiting . . . waiting.

". . . So, what are we going with?"

". . . The bread."

"We're going with the bread."

"Okay . . . you tell him."

And then they turn to Jesus and say,

"It's because we didn't bring any bread, isn't it?"

And then I saw Jesus holding his head in his hands and muttering, "Oh, God" (in the truest sense). "These buffoons are the foundation of a new kingdom?"

This was a great discovery for me; it made sense to me to ask, "Where is the human story in this larger story?" And because of my work in comedy, my most important questions were: Where is that human story funny? And where does the humor and laughter take us into a deeper understanding of the story and the text?

I performed a monologue for my preaching final based on this idea. It was a big hit, and was the genesis of the play Lee and I became most known for—*Fish-Eyes*.

Finally, a reason to be in seminary!

❧ ❧ ❧

Each year I was in school, usually over Christmas vacation, Sue and I would meet with the primary sponsoring couples of our financial support team back home in Lansdale, Pennsylvania. At one such dinner I excitedly told the couples this remarkable artistic discovery I had made, relating my acting experience, giving them my best version of the preaching final, plus the warm response to that final—and seeing a look of . . . a look of . . . what *was* that exactly?

Disappointment?

Irritation?

Frustration?

Apparently, finding the humor in the Bible wasn't quite what they had paid good money for. This was the beginning of a precarious relationship with our support team, as I was obviously veering off the tracks here.

A few years later one of the men attended the same wedding as Sue and me. After the ceremony we were chatting, and he made a comment referencing the service and sermon delivered by someone who had, in fact, graduated from seminary, stayed true to his call, and become a traditional pastor.

"Now that's ministry." (Subtext: that pastor was doing *real* ministry, in contrast to what I was doing.)

SCENE 3

Starting a Theater

IN 1991, WHILE I was still in seminary, Barbra Graber and I formed a group of actors in response to an invitation from the Mennonite Church, to perform at Oregon 91, the denominational assembly: five shows as a late-night option for adults and youth. We formed Theater Akimbo. The name was Lee's idea—it means "from a different angle."

We brought pieces to the group as options to perform and developed others in rehearsal: a couple of dance pieces, musical sketches, and comedy, mostly original with the group. Lee and I were particularly insistent that all the work be original, and all but two pieces were.

The group included Pam Frey, Joy McIlvaine, Duane and Nancy Sider, Suzanne Kiblinger, Jeremy Frey, Sue Swartz, and Lee and me. Barbra directed, I assisted, and Cheryl Zook was tech director. [19]

Lee and I brought "Hold Up"—performed by Lee and Jeremy, where a man was held up at "bookpoint":

"You're holding me up with a book!"

"This isn't just any book."

"Right, it's a magnum—a magnum opus."

"It's a *Sing and Rejoice*" (*a Mennonite-produced songbook, thought by many to be a little lightweight*).

"What are you doing with a *Sing and Rejoice*?"

"I'll sing from it."

"Sing what?"

"'This Is the Day.'"

"Oh, I hate that song."

"I might even sway while singing and perhaps sing it antiphonally."

"You can't do that—you're only one person!"

The "criminal" (Jeremy) then began to sing, and sway, and Lee in desperation gave him his wallet.

One of my favorite sketches was "Twerps." Lee and I walked across stage, meeting in the middle. We were both carrying another actor on our shoulders. I had Jeremy and Lee had Sue, the two lightest cast members. They curled up in balls as tightly as they

---

19 Of course I wanted to Lee to be involved in the Akimbo project, but again he had to be convinced to go along. I found minutes from a planning meeting where several actors' exuberance was evident: "Pam, Jeremy, Joy, Suzanne are in!" However, Lee's response was a bit less so: "Lee thought it sounded like it could be fun."

could, and we carried them out like those big water cooler bottles. The dialogue:

"Ted!"

"Lee!"

"I see you got one too."

"Yeah, where did you get yours?"

"Classifieds."

"Right."

"You?"

"Yard sale." (*And then I would slap Jer on the butt.*)

Exit.

End of bit.[20]

An endearing and enduring memory is the mantra Jeremy would begin muttering after he hopped up on the table on stage right and curled himself into a ball so I could hoist him up onto my shoulder:

"You got me? You got me? You got me? You got me?" He was nervous I would drop him. I asked Lee if Sue ever expressed concern.

"Nope."

A trusting woman, that Sue.

Lee and I loved the silliness of the piece, and the commitment it took. Much of what made Monty Python and early Saturday Night Live brilliant was intelligence coupled with complete commitment to the silly. That's why they were heroes to so many of us.

---

20 About the word *bit*—if it's not long enough to be a sketch, it can be a bit, or piece. I'm not sure of the delineation of when a bit becomes a sketch, or when a sketch becomes a one-act play. I only know for sure that none of them are skits. Why not? A skit indicates amateur—fine for summer camp, but not professional theater.

The cast voted on the sketches and songs to include. And interestingly for Lee and me, a couple of "rejections" turned out to be our favorites—"Bill in the Booth" and "Cathartic Café"—which we put in our first full-length show.

My sketch, "Urinal Etiquette," created a bit of controversy, but we learned a valuable lesson through it: when men face front to demonstrate the proper urinal stance, it's not nearly as funny as when their backs are to the audience—a change we made later. It really did make all the difference. These are the comedy lessons that careers are based on.

```
It is considered uncouth to begin any actual
preparation before assuming the proper urinal
stance, feet approximately shoulder length
apart, weight slightly on the toes, hands
. . . poised.

Distance away of course may vary.

After establishing the target area and per-
haps testing the drainage with expectora-
tion (insert the clearing of the throat and
sounds of spitting), social mores dictate
that the eyes be straight ahead, focusing on
an unseen point or adopting the glazed look
of the unfocused. If, on the rare occasion,
conversation occurs, the head may be slightly
inclined toward the conversationalist but the
unfocused gaze must be maintained. It is also
considered impolite to reach any depth of
interaction at the urinal. . . .
```

The variety of styles and subject matter the show encompassed were fun for the company. We gave ourselves wholly to the concept of "Twerps" and correct posture at the urinal but brought the Bible in as well.

I offered my monologue from seminary, "The Disciples."

Barbra suggested we rewrite for three: Pam, Jeremy, and me. We disciples were yet unnamed. I suppose I was John, because "You talk to him, he likes you best" was a line in the sketch, and John's reputation was as the "disciple Jesus loved"—as if Jesus felt somewhat ambivalent about all the others.

There was a time during rehearsal when I told Barbra I was going to withdraw it because I felt there was a general under-appreciation for the importance of the piece from the younger members of the cast. To me it was too important to make it into a joke piece. The humor lay in the reactions to Jesus, not in making fun of the fact that there was a Jesus. It wasn't a place to question the relevance of Christian faith, but rather to assume a faith and find the human place within that holy story. We had a discussion; the cast agreed that the piece was not about satire, and in the end they put their whole selves into the act. That sketch was a huge hit. Thank you, Pam and Jeremy—your contribution is still felt.

Within two years of meeting Lee, I, my wife Sue, and others discovered what it was like to relate to a person with a bipolar illness—to witness clinical depression up close.

I didn't know what it was at the time. What I did know was my friend could alternately move the world with his creative genius one day, and the next be unable to get out of bed and function as a human being. It was terrifying, and it left me feeling helpless. Twenty years ago I didn't have the tools, or the knowledge.

It became a cruel and ultimate irony. This brilliant comedic actor, this caring, gentle man—who so easily made me laugh, who made me feel good about being alive—had profound doubts about his own worth.

The manic stages of Lee's illness were spectacular. He talked about running the entire communications department at EMU, created long, rambling treatises on the state of the world and faith, wrote an infamous taped opus entitled Carrot Walk—*eating carrots while embarking on a long walk through the neighborhood. It was a mean-*

dering verbal journey, bouncing from one subject to another, while crunching carrots into the microphone. It was while listening to this that people began to wonder about the stability of Lee's mind.

It became another character in our lives—the illness, the depression. A beast, always around the corner, lurking, affecting working relationships, romances, creativity, writing. It came to a head in the fall of 1990 when he entered the hospital. From there he was transferred to a facility in Rockville, Maryland. It seemed whatever hope we had of continuing our stage relationship was gone.

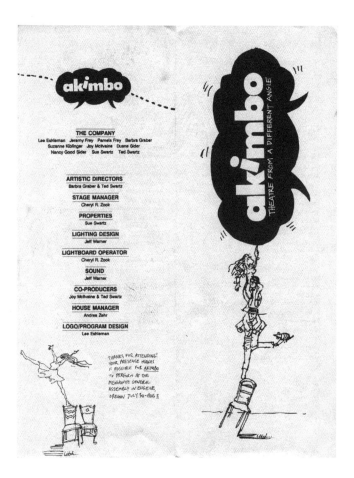

Lee was still living in Rockville, Maryland, under outpatient care. His illness was under control, to the point that he was working as a server in a restaurant. He was the perfect waiter: meticulous, funny, and desperate to please. Customers would request him when dining at the establishment.

His ambivalence and illness were powerful elements. While I knew at this point that I would be doing something with theater, I wasn't as convinced that Lee would be a part of it.

In this project, as with most events, Lee was reluctant, but once he was committed he was fully engaged. He designed the whimsical programs, named the group, was a primary writer, and—of course—was brilliant onstage. But the illness was an elephant in the room.

During rehearsal for "Looks at Books: Cinderella," Barbra pushed us to discover what was under the surface of two characters, Nigel and Neville. They were obviously close, despite being antagonists onstage, their repartee in sketches spoke of a long history—a long co-dependence, if not friendship.

Lee wasn't shy about using his own experience in his writing and acting.

The beginning of "Looks at Books" included these lines:

NIGEL: There will be no such meandering on Looks at Books.

NEVILLE: Why is that, Nigel?

NIGEL: I have been in therapy.

NEVILLE: Excellent.

NIGEL: My name is Nigel and I am a wordaholic.

Barbra wanted to go a bit deeper into the relationship between Nigel and Neville. Who were they to each other? What does it mean to impose our own lives onto these characters? She asked, "How did you feel, Ted, when Lee went into the hospital?"

He and I had never talked about it; perhaps it's just what men do or don't do. Maybe I was simply reverting to my own inability to verbalize appreciation or love. It's always easier to hug someone than tell them how I feel—you're just supposed to infer all of how I feel from the ease with which I touch you. Please don't tell Dr. Phil.

When Barbra asked the question it released all of the pain, concern, helplessness, and love inside, and I just wept. I couldn't talk. Lee put his arms around me as I cried, feeling incapable of stopping; we suspended rehearsal. He seemed to know what I was saying in my grief and helplessness.

Lee and I never really talked about that moment, and we never revisited the "depth question" for these two characters we invented and infused with ourselves. Lee and I felt the comedy would hold up just fine without over-analyzing the characters.

Life with Lee was a joy and a burden. His depression affected relationships, including ours, obviously. But it was just part of the package you got with Lee. You got his genius, his heart, his giftedness in art—but you also got that large land-based mammal in the room.

Ideas:
Where Do They Come From?

MANY TIMES PEOPLE ask, "Where do ideas come from?" As if there is a different gene inside the heads of creative people. Comedic ideas often come when your eyes and ears are open to the possibility that every moment has potential for comedy. It's not making fun of life—it's celebrating life. Occasionally, to their chagrin, our boys were subject matter for sketches or monologues. This was a monologue in response to a difficult culinary experience for Eliot.

ELIOT AND THE EDGES

It was my turn to make supper that fateful night. I had chosen to make . . . an omelet.

Broccoli, potatoes, onion, ham, one dozen eggs, and melted cheese—truly a delight. I couldn't help but admire the golden sea of eggs dotted with islands of lovingly prepared vegetables and spices.

And there, because of added heat and extra margarine, the outsides browned and curled, creating a border of different colors. It was beautiful.

So it was with great optimism that I slid the dish across the table; surely this would be met with approval and even applause.

For I had seen those curled and browned outsides as delightful.

Eliot, age six, saw them as . . . different. So while the other boys and I dug in, he sat.

"Dad, what's this?"

"Why son, that's an omelet, just the way you like it, with all the stuff in it."

"No, what's this?"

Now I saw where he was pointing, fear in his eyes.

"Oh, Eliot, that's just where the extra margarine made the edges curl up."

"There're edges?" he asked.

"Yes, edges."

He sat in silence.

"What's the matter, son?"

"I can't eat this. I've never eaten this before."

"Of course you can, of course you have; it isn't any different than any other omelet I've made."

You see, despite my better intentions, a bite had entered my voice. "Every single omelet I've made and you've eaten has had an edge on it. Every single omelet that's ever lived has had an edge."

Tears began to form in his eyes.

"Eliot, there is no difference! What is the
problem?"

"I'm afraid."

"Afraid?! Of what?"

Knowing I was to leave for a play rehearsal
within the hour, I took the opportunity to
warm up and work on my diction. "Eliot, these
. . . are the very same eggs that I've always
made, the only difference is in the color and
possibly the texture of the outermost region
of . . . said . . . eggs."

He was unchanged in his terror of the evil
omelet. His only explanation was, "I've never
eaten edges before."

I learned two important lessons that day: You
can't make an omelet without an edge, and
those edges can be pretty scary stuff when
you're six.

Perhaps edges are always a little scary. Edges of omelets, edges
of faith, edges of society.

"Bill in the Booth"

The winter Lee was hospitalized we had been booked to perform
at Eastern Mennonite College. Now without Lee, I was on solo
for a thirty-minute show, and I was scrambling for material. As I
paced around my office, I noticed the basketball encyclopedia on
the bookshelf next to the complete works of William Shakespeare.
One formula for creating comedy is juxtaposition, putting two
things together that ordinarily don't belong—for example, basketball and Shakespeare. That could be funny. That night I wrote,
"Bill in the Booth: William Shakespeare Does the Play-by-Play
and Color Commentary of a Professional Basketball Game":

Three minutes hence to our conclude. Spurs have the lead: 85-84.

while Detroit controlleth the ball.

But ho, Anderson doth steal it hence.

O you knave. O thou pernicious caitiff.

You are naught, you are naught, I'll mark this play.

For this perchance a turning point.

Posthaste he doth bring the ball fore court,

Sir William there is some post to us or thee, dost thou seeth him?

Robinson is open underneath.

But ho e'en whilst the ball is yet on route,

Rodmen, whither has he come?

What ho, a foul, I say.

With arms encumbered thusly, yet does he still score,

the bucket and one more.

88-84.

Dumars taketh yet another pass

and perchance to drive the lane.

But in his path there riseth one David Robinson

to swat asunder yon eliptic orb.

What, are you mad? I charge you, get you home.

```
Take that weak stuff out of town.
```

. . . and so on.

Accumulating "inventory"

In the spring of 1992 Lee and I were asked to perform at a storytelling conference. There we worked up a piece where two characters would communicate only with thought bubbles they would cut out and scribble on. This developed into "When Shrimp Learn to Whistle," a clowning routine where Lee asked in a thought bubble he cut out:

"?" (In other words, *What's up?*)

I pulled a scissors from my briefcase and cut out a dollar sign.

Lee cut out a knife.

I cut out a sword.

Lee cut out a gun.

I cut out a bigger gun.

Machine gun.

Bomb.

Missile.

Which I didn't have an answer for, and in a panic I simply cut off the end of the missile, sending it spiraling to the ground, a nuclear warhead circumcision.

We slammed our briefcases shut and raised fists, which morphed into a rock/paper/scissors game resulting in a tie: two pairs of scissors. Stalemate. The characters then slunk off.

The audience loved the broad comic sensibilities, and people told us, "That was funny, but . . . We got it."

Got what? we thought. *We're just doing stuff we think is funny . . . we're not trying . . . Oooohhhh, the escalation of armaments to an end in which no one wins. Oh sure, that's what we meant all along.*

At that same conference we were asked to create a piece from a biblical story, John 21—a Jesus story, post-crucifixion and post-resurrection. Again we asked ourselves, "What is interesting or funny?"—usually the same thing. The comedy was in the image of a couple of Jesus' disciples, discouraged and depressed while fishing and having Jesus verbally accost them from the shore, asking somewhat facetiously, "Have you caught anything?" We figured Jesus had to be hard to understand—if he was shouting from several hundred yards away.

PETER: Andy, who's that on the shore?

ANDREW: I don't know. But he's hollering at us.

BOTH: WHAAAAAAAAAAAAT!!!!!!!!!????????

PETER: Have we caught anything?

ANDREW: Oh, ha ha ha. Aren't you the funny one, you halibut heckler.

BOTH: NOOOOOOO!

(*They turn away, then hear the call again.*)

BOTH: WHAAAAAAAAATTTT?

ANDREW: Caaaaa . . . Caaa . . . Cashew. Nuts. Cashew nuts. Cashew nuts on the other side. Cashew nuts?

PETER: Cashew nuts?

ANDREW: Did you bring a snack?

PETER: No, I didn't bring one.

BOTH: WHAAAAAAAAAAAAT?!

ANDREW: Caaaa . . . caaaaa . . .

PETER: Here he goes again . . .

ANDREW: CAST! Okay, second word. (*gives a charades symbol*) You . . . you . . . your . . .

PETER: He's talking about us . . .

This piece was to become the final scene of *Fish-Eyes*.[21]

A lump under the rug of my heart—and other stimulating overheard conversations that we formed into a show . . .

Sue and I went to a Marriage Encounter weekend in early 1991. Marriage Encounter is an organization started within the Catholic Church, and copied by many other denominations. Ours was a Mennonite version, meeting an hour up the road at the Quality Inn and Johnny Appleseed Restaurant in New Market, Virginia. The encounters were structured around stories told by the leaders.

I suppose it was a good weekend away for Sue and me. However, we were quite irreverent. We laughed a lot, and not always at the things we were supposed to be laughing about. Sometimes structured activities designed to elicit creative dialogue between spouses strike me—and at this weekend, Sue—the wrong way.

One of the couples, with great honesty and vulnerability, related the story of one of them buying a piece of furniture without telling the other. For them, it was a major problem; to us, it didn't seem like much of a big deal, perhaps because we didn't have any money to spend, either illicitly or with full disclosure.

After the inevitable confrontation, there were still things left unsaid. The wife, reading her story, said the fact that her husband had withheld information felt like there was "a lump under the rug of my heart." Sue and I both choked and sputtered, trying not to make a scene. It must have been a vivid visual picture of the pain she was in. It certainly stuck in our heads.

I, of course, told Lee. He and I were in Wayne G.'s room at

---

21 The resource person for the weekend was storyteller Rosella Regier. Fifteen years later, in Newton, Kansas, we were performing a retrospective of our work, related this story, and noticed Rosella was in the audience. We noted and applauded her—and on the way out after curtain call, we veered toward Rosella, sank to our knees before her, kissed her hand, and exited with a flourish. Had we capes, we would have swirled them.

Bridgewater College—perhaps to look at some photos Wayne had taken. Lee threw out another phrase that almost sounded like a cliché, or a wise saying. Almost. That was the beginning of "Steel Girders," a sketch created for our first full show, *Armadillo Tour*, in 1992. Two steelworkers balanced on a girder seventeen stories up, eating lunch and musing about their boss:

RUDY: Now, you may not see wok to hubcap with me on this one, but that new foreman, he gives me a weasel under the carpet feeling, you know what I'm talkin' about?

FRANK: I hear ya, now I'm not the kind of guy to buy a gumball with a twenty dollar bill, mind you.

RUDY: I know that.

FRANK: But when he promises a pay hike, I think he's just fishin' for axles through the screen door.

RUDY: Well, I'm not the sort of guy to flush the john with two hands, but he strikes me as a photograph-the-back-of-the-camera sorta guy.

FRANK: A hedgehog on helium.

RUDY: A roving parenthetical expression just waiting to pitch a tent . . . Now mind you, you tell me if I'm just fluffin' the cactus on this one, but I think he's just a squealin' bagpipe just itchin' to bury the coffee.

FRANK: Well, Rudy, why don't we just shave the monkey and see what the wizard writes home about—'cause I'm not the kind of guy to wear a cashmere sweater and ride a unicycle up the side of a cathedral hummin' Patsy Kline songs through my nose.

(*Pause.*)

Then again, every dog has his day.

RUDY: What?

FRANK: I said every dog has his day.

RUDY: Now, what does that mean? Sometimes you make no sense at all.

FRANK: (*falling from the girder*) AAAAAAHHHH-hhhhhhhhhh.

And then Frank (Lee) falls from the girder, rising up to simulate a "poof" as he hits the ground.

RUDY: (*breaking character*) I guess the building ain't so high after all . . . Bob, this ain't workin'! They don't believe we're sev-

Soon after the show, when Lee was back in Rockville, I received a letter from him, complete with drawings of Frank and Rudy on the envelope.

enteen stories up here. I mean, you can fool
some of the people some of the time, but you
cannot bounce a potato chip off the *Mona
Lisa*. Am I right, Frank?

FRANK: I believe that's right.

One of my favorite memories of that two-week run was watching Bob Small, director of the show, in the back of the room, shrugging in delighted response, as if to say, "Whatta ya gonna do?" to our plea, "Bob, this ain't workin'!" It was our little moment as actors to include him in the show.

SCENE 5

Ted & Lee Live:
The Armadillo Tour

IN 1992 LEE and I developed our first full-length comedy show: *Ted & Lee Live, the Armadillo Tour.* We didn't have a differentiated company name, but we decided the "Live" alliterated with Lee, so Ted came first—*Ted and Lee Live.* A deep reason for a monumental decision: whose name comes first. And the brand Ted & Lee was birthed.

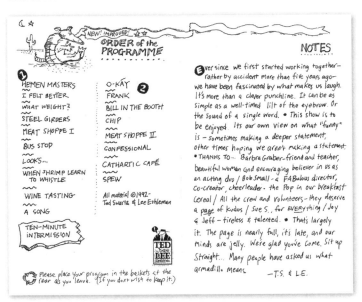

Program from *Armadillo Tour* 1992.

At the time, we were still affiliated with Akimbo, the company Barbra and I had formed in '91. Barbra didn't feel she was the one to direct this brand of humor, so she asked her friend Bob Small to join us. That began a relationship that has lasted for twenty years. Bob has had a hand in dramaturging or directing nine of the shows I have written or cowritten. We came with about half of the material written; the other half was improv-ed and then scripted. A great memory is Bob's braying staccato laughter at the end of a sketch. Bob even laughs in beats of three: there's a beginning, a middle, and an end.

Armadillo Tour was where Zeus the homeless man originated, Lee's iconic Nigel Nevillson flowered, and "Spew" debuted. "Cathartic Café," "Bill in the Booth," "He-Men Wrestlers of Ballet," "Chip," "Steel Girders," and "Meat Shoppe"[22] all got their starts in that show.

Final rehearsal on Wednesday night before opening was horrible. The show was too long, and some of the pieces we just were not happy with. We were also suffering from the dreaded "too-much-time-in-a-comedy-without-an-audience" syndrome.

Most artists live under what I call a constant low-grade fear of irrelevance. Your next bomb is just around the corner; you are only as funny or relevant as your latest work; and to proclaim, "This show will be funny!" and then feel that nothing is working theatrically or comedically is terrifying.

Bob sat us down and asked us what we thought. We both felt the same: we weren't ready—for the next night, for two weeks of shows, to be onstage as professionals in the first place.

He reassured us we were funny, that the show had some problems we needed to fix, but we had a show. It would work. We were still funny.

We were still funny! Thanks, Dad, we needed that.

Barbra, acting as producer for the show, had this to say about it:

---

22 This is where I used my meat-cutting knowledge to describe various cuts of beef, even including an actual quote from my grandfather in response to the bone being included in the cut: "When you buy the land you buy the stone, when you buy the meat . . . you buy the bone."

"It is refreshing and heartwarming to see a comedy show that doesn't demean women and, as well, reveals two men who honestly care about each other." We hadn't realized we were pouring our relationship into the material—it was merely the material we felt drawn to write.

In the midst of the comedy we inserted two monologues we called "the serious pieces" (not especially creative references, but working titles tend toward simplicity).

The first one I wrote while in Advanced Acting class at James Madison University, after Professor Tom Arthur told me the story of visiting his aging mother. I was moved by his account and went home and rewrote it as a monologue. At the next class period I asked him if I could make it my final monologue project.

ON WITH IT

My mother has Alzheimer's disease. Last time I was there I watched her take three dishes out of the refrigerator and open them one by one . . .

But by the time she'd opened the third, she had forgotten what was in the first . . .

So she started over—discovering what was in those same three dishes.

And it was funny and it hurt and it was funny but she did it for twenty minutes. And after twenty minutes I wanted to strangle her. . .

. . . my own mother . . .

. . . my mother, who has a PhD.

She looked at me, with the Tupperware lid in her hand and said, "D***, I can't remember, but I know why I can't remember and I hate knowing why."

And then she said, "I just wish it would get on with it so I won't know why . . . and it won't matter."

And I know there will come a time when she won't know who I am and then I'll wish it would just get on with it. . . .

❚ ❚ ❚

Lee contributed a personal story, well-crafted and delivered, but haunting in its honesty.

CHICKEN

Not too long ago, I spent some time in the hospital.

On the mental floor.

The loony bin.

I'd gotten kind of depressed.

Well, not kind of—actually very depressed to the point of having a death wish . . . you know, hoping I wouldn't wake up in the morning or plotting to go swimming in a rock quarry and accidentally tiring out.

One July afternoon before I was hospitalized my family was up visiting me and I thought it would be a nice idea to barbecue chicken for everyone. The folks, the brother, the grandparents. I don't know where the energy to try this came from, because when you're depressed, just planning a route to the bathroom seems impossible. It's like moving through motor oil. But I plunged ahead, borrowed a grill . . .

. . . and burned the chicken.

I watched the fat-fed flames cremate my dinner, ruin everything that I had to offer my family, and something snapped. I dropped myself at the foot of a tree and cried like I hadn't cried in a long, long time.

My brother just sat beside me, rubbed my back, and said, "There's no one else in the world like you, there's no one else in the world like you."

I rocked back and forth and thought, "Right. Everyone else knows how to barbecue chicken."

Nigel

If I were to say who Lee's favorite character was, it would easily be Nigel Nevillson—good-hearted, verbose, meandering, out-of-control Nigel.

The first time we performed "Looks at Books" was on EMU's campus, as an addition to a night of scenes from an acting class. We liked the idea of over-analyzing a children's story, and chose "Little Red Riding Hood."

My character, Neville, hated the stories, delighted in exposing the inadequate plots and underdeveloped characters. Lee's character loved them, finding great spiritual meaning in all the stories:

Little Red Riding Hood: "Here the entrance of the woodsman—of course the Christ figure in the story."

NEV: Fast-moving, seamless? You call this flaccid, predictable piece of drivel fast-moving and seamless? The story reads like the cover of a supermarket tabloid, seething with violence, hedonism, and sexual innuendo. Nigel, I'm appalled that in one week we've fallen from discussing Dante's Inferno to prattling on about sensationalist claptrap. I found the senseless violence (which, incidentally, Scarry doesn't have the balls to show us) appellingly unnecessary. The plot was transparent and the characters nauseatingly shallow. The entire work was as limp as Casanova's twelfth night. I was unmoved.

NIG: You do me damage, sir. This tale is not limp, but taut. Taut as the pectorals of Hulk Hogan. Consider the characters—little red riding hood—the picture of philanthropy and purity—balanced against a trusting child-like innocence, which makes her easy prey for the foe, the wolf. And a formidable foe he is—the big bad wolf exhibits a kind of slimy deceit and a zealous appetite for living flesh. It would be tempting to paint such a scoundrel in one-dimensional, harsh strokes, yet our author, recognizing the inherent contradictions of this life, imbues the wolf with a partly redeeming lyricism. A certain verbal sense and Jnin de vivre, if you will, makes his nastiness a bit more palatable. Consider the baptist preacher rhythm and refrain of "all the better to hear you with, my dear" "all the better to see you with, my dear" and then "all the better to EAT you with my dear!" And suddenly he is on her. She screams AUUGH! AUUGH! Enter the lumberjack. Easiely overlooked because of his brief appearance, the lumberjack is of course the Christ figure in the drama. |He hits the wolf on the head! Conk! I'm reminded of Christ clearing the temple or Hercules beheading the Medusa. "Death and Evil", the wolf, falls defeated like a stone-stung Goliath. THUD. (drop too close to Nev's family jewels with hand gesture.) Evil is undone, good triumphs, and supper has not been delayed. A spirited, delightfully simple tale teeming with well-rounded, redemptive characters in an airtight plot. Neville.

First writings of "Little Red Riding Hood."

Cinderella: "A story of redemptive transformation."

Curious George: "God as the man in a yellow hat? And George—curious, a naughty creation—an homage to the delicious and confounding discussion of the evolution/creation debate?"

But our favorite was *Green Eggs and Ham*.

I, as Neville, of course found something amiss. In this case, it was the obvious drug culture running through this subversive work.

NEVILLE: Oh sure, first it starts with green eggs and next Clyde is entrapped in a spiraling abyss of amorphous blue hills, yellow trees, and Casey Jones drivin' that train . . . I wonder when this book was published? Ah! What a coincidence—1960. It seems that the drug-induced haze that was the '60s can be laid firmly at the furry feet of Sam I Am.

Lee as Nigel, found something completely different.

NIGEL: Neville, once again you are passing mental gas. There is majesty in these pages. Let's look at them, shall we?

(*reads*) "I am Sam."

"SAM I AM."

Sam . . . I . . . Am. Hmmm . . . Isn't there someone else, someone else who would nourish us, even when we don't want it? Someone else, tenderly calling us?

"Would you listen here,

would you listen there,

would you listen anywhere?"

Someone who will doggedly pursue us, say-

ing, "These are my eggs, come, take and eat?"
Indeed, Neville, Sam is no pusher, is he?
Isn't Sam, rather, the great I AM? Isn't Sam
. . . the Lord?

NEVILLE: In a word, Nigel—no.

NIGEL: Oh Neville, is there no room in your
heart for little Sam? For only he can hear
our cries in the night, when the crazed mon-
keys of doom have surrounded us, when we are
bent over the boiling cauldron of despair—
only he can hear our still small voice cry-

Early "Looks at Books."

ing out, "We are here, we are here, we are
here!" For only he, only the great I AM
hears our cries and holds us like a mother
would, only the great I AM knows that no
matter who we are, WE ARE WHO! Can I have an
"amen?"

♦ ♦ ♦

The show was a success, drawing increasingly larger crowds
through the last weekend, but most importantly giving us a product that we did . . . nothing with.

We had no gigs through the fall of 1992. We didn't know
how to do a theater business. Lee still wasn't sure this was something he wanted to pursue; I wasn't equipped to drag him into
an endeavor that had no shape. I was dropping into depression.
Through that fall and winter I did odd jobs, some painting, even
spent an afternoon putting prefab furniture together for a family. The guy could have done it himself, I'm sure, but boy, did we
need the money.

So, this decision to spend five years preparing for a career
I immediately discarded as irrelevant was looking like the old
"Swartz business magic" at work again. I thought I had found my
place in life, knew who I was, found the passion of a calling—but I
had absolutely no way to get there. I was thirty-five years old, with
three young sons, a wife who had put in five years supporting me,
and an annoyed congregation back in Pennsylvania waiting for a
return on their investment.

The bold and heartfelt announcement of a new calling and
direction wasn't being heard in quite the same fashion back at
the Plains congregation. It seems what was touching my soul
was a foreign language to the good folks there. They bore a good
amount of confusion and anger toward my decision. It was a very
odd situation. My sense of obligation to their investment, coupled
with my personality of "doing the right thing" was now at odds

with my true self; a self that finally was coming into focus. How could I make a living at acting and writing without moving from Harrisonburg?

BE SURE TO INCLUDE THE ARMADILLO - THE REST IS
OPTIONAL.

SCENE 6

A Large, Bloodied, Exhausting Step Forward

Summer 1993 was Mennonite Convention in Philadelphia. We were asked to present announcements for the youth convention, both morning and evening. Our task was to take mundane announcements about meal times, street crossing safety, changes in schedule, where the 5K run would start—and make them funny. It was guerilla sketch comedy writing.

On one morning we were giving a demonstration of different mammals, squirrels, moles crossing the street, including a Menno youth with his or her head in the clouds. I strolled across the stage and Lee sounded a car horn and I did a dead fall forward as if getting hit by the auto. I was a little overexuberant and tilted forward a tad too far and hit the stage, not in a full body impact, thereby diminishing possible danger, but with my chin. So while Lee finished the announcement with grand aplomb, I noticed I was leaking. There is video record of me dabbing my chin and wiping the blood off on my sock. I had a full beard at the time, and no one (not even Lee) was aware of the accident. After finally locating the first aid station, I accepted four stitches and off we went to the next gig, having learned another valuable lesson in stage craft: don't let the adrenaline of performing in front of six thousand people tilt you too far.

We negotiated to perform *Armadillo Tour* as a late-night option for youth, family, and adult audiences. I was also performing in another play produced by Akimbo, and we were writing comedy routines on the fly before the morning and evening gatherings. After much struggle with the regulatory authorities of the Mennonite Church, we were allowed to charge one dollar for each ninety-minute comedy show that started at ten p.m. After each late-night show, we would tear down and move the set and equipment, get to bed around one or two a.m., then up at six for morning writing and performance. We had tech staff: Sue, Sue Miller, and Joy McIlvaine. By the time we hit midweek, Lee and I were so frazzled, we couldn't remember the directions to the convention center. We would walk out of any one of the hotels in the conference center area, and pause—

Joy or Sue: "Turn right."—and so off we would go, to engage the masses once again in hilarity.

The late-night shows were hits, with good crowds for almost all of the shows. We collected over $1,600 in cash, mostly in precious one-dollar bills, which we stuffed in my briefcase. Leaving the hotel, exhausted but exhilarated, we loaded the luggage, props, and costumes in the trusty VW Vanagon, and pulled onto the mean streets of Philadelphia to head down I-95 to Virginia.

Sue: "Where's the briefcase?"

Ted: "It's not behind the seat?"

Sue: "No."

Frantically around the block in the big bad city, to the parking garage of the Sheraton, and there—where I had left it, on the sidewalk—was my briefcase with all of the earnings for the week.

As we left town, Lee and I scribbled on scrap paper the response, at right, to the week.

In the fall of 1993 we wrangled a week of gigs, up through Holmes County, Ohio, staying at Camp Luz with friends and cousin Kris and Kirk Shank-Zehr. We did shows at Central Christian High School in Kidron, and then out to Goshen College, where we performed *Armadillo Tour* at the Umble Center, one of the best spaces for an actor I've had the privilege of performing in. A favorite memory is the Sylvia and Robert Shirk

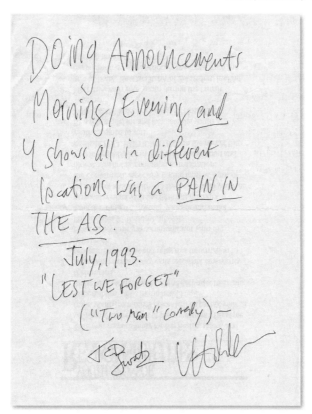

Doing Announcements Morning/Evening and 4 shows all in different locations was a PAIN IN THE ASS.

July, 1993.

"LEST WE FORGET"

("Two Man" comedy) —

Charles family, in the front row, in preparation for the final scene, "Spew!"—all donning rain ponchos.

Q Q Q

The skill I learned the year after the store closed, painting houses, was still coming in handy. I also learned something about my personality through painting: when painting a wall, you need to continue to follow a structure and method: lots of paint on the roller; four to six feet in width at a time; careful work in feathering the edges; keep moving, never stop except at a corner.

Painting woodwork was different for me—especially windows. For some reason, I would start on a corner, and then jump to another corner before the run was finished—perhaps classic

ADHD behavior: "Oh look! Another corner!"

The window would be finished, and finished well, but getting there was not a rational, organized process. Writing a play, a book, a conversation even, is not a rational, organized process for me. However, the play gets done—the book gets done—hopefully well. When asked about my writing process I'll occasionally say, "It's like painting a window." Hmm . . . deep, mysterious, yes, very true, a window, yes, I can see that.

No, no you can't.

SCENE 7

Fish-Eyes

IN THE WINTER of 1994, Jerry Holsopple[23] and Allen Angell from Mennonite Media came to us with a proposal: a video curriculum based on the stories we had begun developing on the disciples of Jesus—fourteen episodes. A writing grant of $6,000 was secured, and we embarked on the project, not really knowing how to write for video or, quite frankly, this much material. We also decided the full-length stage show would be created at the same time; in response to the grant, we would do a benefit premier of the show in March. It was a ridiculous amount of creativity output, especially considering our lack of video experience.

Before starting the disciple show, we had the end (the lakeshore scene after the resurrection, written in '92) and the middle of the show, developed out of the three-person "Disciples" sketch (first performed in '91).

After six weeks, we performed the first reading with a few trusted friends—Barbra Graber, Cheryl Zook, Jerry, Wayne Gehman, and Duane Sider. The response was positive overall. At this point in development, I was John and Lee was Andrew, both fishermen but unrelated to one another.

Duane, in a moment of brilliance, said, "You act like brothers; (motioning to me) why aren't you Peter?"

Lee and I looked at each other.

"Well, duh."

---

23 It was Jerry who coined the title *Fish-Eyes*.

The show took a strong turn from that pivotal observation. Peter's character grew with a cynical, gruff, passionate energy, while Lee's Andrew blossomed with bright personality and tender quirks.[24] Andrew was an artist, cared about the aesthetic of the moment, was verbal and witty, a tad naive with a perception that humans are intrinsically good. While I drove the writing process, Lee wrote a great monologue reflecting another view of Judas.

```
I don't think I'm crazy or anything. It's
not me anyway. It's him. He's the one that
upsets me. He was supposed to get me out,
away from all those women batting their eye-
lashes and the gamblers and the dirty beg-
gars, he was gonna save me. But he talks to
them, he looks at them, he touches them . . .
he touches them. One of these days he's going
catch something. The great healer to swallow
too much dirt, and his beautiful hand will
fall off in a shower of white flakes or some
pig demon's gonna go run right up his nose.
I dream he walks across the water again and
there are two of me there on shore and he
signals me, come . . . come to me, he says.
So I walk to him, he takes our hands and as
he does, one of me peels off and sinks to the
bottom like a stone. He just watches it sink.
He doesn't try to save it. I try to be good,
but I'm not. It's not like I don't want to
be good. I just don't feel like I can ever
change. Sometimes I just can't take it. Some-
times I wish I had never been born.
```

---

24 During the writing and study for the show, we noted that according to the text, Peter swore during the denial scene. Our script: "D*** it, I said I don't know this man! Why don't you people just leave me the h*** alone?!" After a couple of years, we grew tired of certain audiences fixating on the language and not the story and withdrew our interpretation of literal interpretation.

We knew we had something, something different within the field of "faith-based theater using comedy to find a deeper meaning within a familiar story." Oh, you're saying that's a very small field? Well, so be it.

Sequence from Virginia premier of *Fish-Eyes*, which sold out 900-plus seats.

In the summer of '95, while the show was still pretty fresh, we were in a conference in Wichita, performing *Fish-Eyes*. The crew was the union crew for the theater in the conference center—including Rocky, the chain smoking, nominally agnostic, cynical lighting tech. After the show, Rocky delivered one of our favorite comments ever regarding *Fish-Eyes*:

"Guys, that was pretty f***ing entertaining."

Well, thanks Rocky; we probably can't use that in our promotional material, but thanks.

One of early posters for *Fish-Eyes* had us posing with props, using our default facial expressions: Lee with his imposing eyebrow raised on top of his imposing height; me using the broad smile that forced my mustache into a parallel line with my eyebrows. Lee turned this photo into a caricature for use on a different promotional piece. He was showing me the work when Derek, age seven, wandered through.

"Can I see?"

"Sure."

(Pause.)

"Huh, Dad's cheeks look too fat and you look like you're wearing a mask."

" . . . Okay."

"Is that the best you can do?"

❦ ❦ ❦

Lee as Andrew was rarely without his sketchbook in the show—it became a strong personality choice. Peter was the disciple we thought we knew best, because of the numerous biblical references to his impulsive, volatile nature. Andrew was a more open slate for Lee to create his own interpretation. One of our favorite scenes was "The Last Supper," where Andrew tries to convince Peter he has a great plan for seating for the evening. Peter resists, asking, "What do you mean, this isn't how you picture it?"

ANDREW: I was hoping you'd ask. (produces a sketch in his sketchbook) I've been working on this all day. It's a little seating chart for dinner. Where people sit, what elements we use, the whole shebang.

PETER: With suggested facial expressions and hand gestures I see. Andy you got us all sitting in a line here. I hate that. You can't talk to anybody when you sit in a line. And what's this—these architectural lines converging dramatically in a vanishing point behind his head. What's that? This place doesn't look like that.

ANDREW: I know. Dramatic effect.

PETER: Dramatic effect. What's this disc behind his head? What's that thing?

ANDREW: That's a symbol.

PETER: Andy, you drew him with a beard. He doesn't have a beard.

ANDREW: I know.

PETER: You know? He doesn't have long hair either. He hates it. Gets all tangly.

ANDREW: I know.

PETER: You know?

ANDREW: Of course. I just like to draw him
this way. I think it might catch on. . . .

    During the course of the scene Lee would show me the layout
in his sketchbook—whenever he got the urge, he would quickly
sketch a new version of Da Vinci's *The Last Supper*. But he would
usually give me a surprise, eliciting stifled laughter as I would try to
move on, in an effort to ignore the special guests Lee would draw
into the scene.

Becoming professionals

By the fall of 1995, I was becoming aware of my inadequacies of running the office while being on the road. This was before cell phones or remote email, and we sensed we were missing opportunities while being away from the home phone.

We asked Sheri Hartzler if she would like to be our agent. She wasn't really sure what that would entail, and neither were we. But she was smart, organized, focused, and great with people. Those seemed like attributes of a good agent—and it turned out we were right.

Sheri learned the business and we began to do more of what we did best—write and act. She was and is fiercely loyal. She probably heard too much of me complaining about Lee, and probably too much of Lee complaining about me. She wonderfully negotiated the terrain between friend and colleague, while also honoring the friendships with Sue and Lee's wife, Reagan—scheduling us out, but not too much. She was ballast for our personalities, editor, confidante, agenda creator, consultant, and the hardest worker any of us ever met. Lee and I would sometimes tell people on the road we were actually working for Sheri. We were hoping to do a good job so we wouldn't get fired one day. Now we could say, "If you would call our agent . . ." or "I was just talking to our agent . . ." or "I'm sorry, I can't give you a quote on that project, you'll have to . . . call our agent."

So now we were traveling professionals, sometimes feeling like frauds, sometimes feeling like we belonged. But I felt like I was right where I was supposed to be. When asked about how one starts a business like ours, my simple answer was, "naive persistence"—the same as getting married young. I hadn't realized this was going to be this hard, but didn't doubt it should happen. Lee never quite shared the same resolve, the absolute conviction, because he didn't necessarily feel conviction about anything. For him, it was a good time, he was very good at it, we liked being together—mostly—and so it made sense for the moment.

SCENE 8

DoveTale: Writing a Christmas Show in Which Rehearsals Look and Smell Better

OUR CONGREGATION WAS a crucial part of our lives and also contributed to the development of me as an artist. For four consecutive years, with a group of volunteers, I wrote an Advent sketch for the church. We would meet four weeks out, read the Scripture, and then respond to four basic questions:

1. What was interesting? Not what does this mean, but rather, what piqued your interest?

2. What was different? These Advent stories were so familiar; occasionally the little detail that pokes at us was the start of a sketch.

3. What was funny? Usually we didn't need a lot of encouragement to find the humor; we are hungry for it, look for it—the trick for writers is to craft that fun idea sprouting up spontaneously into a coherent script that recaptures the elusive mystical element that made us laugh in the first place.

4. Where's the conflict? We need to have a conflict to keep our interest. Once good followers of the Prince of Peace

understand that theater needs it, they are real good at finding conflict.

At the end of four years of this process, I had the beginnings of
what I would bring to the writing of *DoveTale*, our Christmas play.

DoveTale is a Christmas show Lee and I created with Ingrid
De Sanctis in 1997. Ingrid was in college with Lee and actually
overlapped with me for a year and semester. Everyone on campus
knew who Ingrid was: a great actor who happened to be beautiful
as well. We were friends during my college years, but not especially
close. It was when she moved back to Harrisonburg to teach at
EMU that we began writing together and dreaming about creating
shows together. We toured *DoveTale* for ten years together, and
looked forward to it each December. Ingrid said it was a favorite
time of the year for her—deepening friendships while doing what
we loved.

The writing of the show, however, was not always beloved. It's
hard enough to write with two; three became a real exercise in
compromise, patience, grace, and love. Ingrid and I were passionate about our ideas and wanted them to work. We were also trying
to establish ourselves as writers, so ego and control were at stake.
(Incidentally, these two dragons of insecurity have probably sunk
far more creative projects than any amount of lack of funding ever
did.)

Lee . . . Lee just wanted us to all get along.

Once, during a trip to Tennessee, Ingrid and I finally had it
out—in the middle of a Books-A-Million store. We finally aired
our hurts and anger at our perceived lack of appreciation and
respect for each other as artists. We can laugh about it now, due in
large part to Lee's role in the episode.

Ingrid's sister, Kathy, is a close confidante of Ing's, and they talk
often. After leaving the Books-A-Million,[25] while the air was still
crackling with tension, Lee pulled out his phone and whispered

---

25 Ingrid thinks it was a Barnes and Noble, not a Books-A-Million. It wasn't.

urgently, his voice filled with horror, "Kath, it's Lee . . . They're fighting again, Ted and Ingrid. What should I do? . . . No, no, I tried that . . . I tried that . . . I tried that. Do you think I should let either one drive? . . . Okay. Do you think they'll try to kill each other? . . . No, no, I took Ingrid's gun earlier today; she was shooting out the window."

We almost hurt ourselves laughing at him.

While Ingrid and I needed to (and did) talk through our stuff, it sure didn't hurt having Lee create a comedy routine out of our relationship.

An interesting aspect of any play is the question, "Whose play is it?" Meaning, which character drives the arc of the play, who is the one the audience is most strongly drawn to emotionally, who is the caretaker of the audience's experience? We discovered it was Lee's character, Gabriel, who filled that role in *DoveTale*. He moved the play along; he was the audience's confidant, the ringmaster to the unveiling of the story.

From Gabriel, he jumped to Jean Claude, the arrogant stuffy waiter; to the lounge singer Arny Pufkin; to Leo the wedding photographer ("Joseph's cousin, twice removed—once against my will"); and a special treat for me: a cameo from Nigel Nevillson, playing the innkeeper.

NIGEL: Good evening and welcome. Ordinarily it would be welcome, I mean, but of course there are no vacancies. There appears to be a huge Parcheesi convention going on across town. Lots of shake, rattle, and roll going on, don't you know, from the deck to the vestibule. I'm reminded of a story. It seems that I and a few of the old cronies from the war were tenting in Bethesda . . .

JOSEPH: (*interrupting*) Excuse me. Sir, do you have anything? This is the ninth inn we've been to.

MARY: (*yelling from down right*) Do you have a room yet?!

JOSEPH: We've been on the road for what seems like a year.

(*Mary keeps interrupting and yelling to Joseph while he is talking with Nigel at the door.*)

MARY: Ask him if they provide breakfast.

JOSEPH: Do you have anything at all?

MARY: And if the kitchen's still open.

JOSEPH: My wife is tired; she's pregnant.

NIGEL: (*Nigel looks over at Mary.*) That's true; she seems to be absolutely fabulous with child. But as I've said there just isn't room in the inn.

(*Mary screams. The others freeze. Mary screams again and is going into labor.*)

JOSEPH: We're gonna need some hot water!
(*Joseph crosses to Mary.*)

NIGEL: Ah! Hot water, excellent idea, tea.
Tea is a calming influence . . . a nice herbal
blend . . .

DoveTale became one of our most popular works. For ten years we performed between six and ten shows each December, an opportunity to reacquaint ourselves with favorite characters. When you get the chance only once a year, it's like reuniting with an old friend you hadn't seen in eleven months.[26]

Take it

"Take it . . . take it . . . take it," I whispered to Lee as he walked off stage left, leaving me "asleep onstage" as Joseph. It was the eighth season of *DoveTale*, and we'd come to the part where Gabriel, in a dream, is supposed to take a baby out of Joseph's arms.

Context: In the end of the first act the angel Gabriel comes to Joseph in a dream and tells him to "marry Mary." In our version, Gabriel becomes a professional wrestler and throws Joseph around the stage. In the first couple seasons he threw Joe over the couch, but we found it much more fun to have him thrown off the front of the stage, whereupon I (Joe) would seek refuge among the audience members—with varying degrees of acceptance. I would usually try to find a woman with a kind face to "give me refuge" from the bad man onstage. At one point within Joseph's dream, after he returns to the stage, Mary appears onstage and hands him a baby, which he doesn't want, protests that he can't do this, it's not his.

He protests until he opens the blanket and looks at the child, mesmerized. Gabriel steers him back to the couch and into the

---

26 I received this email a couple of years ago from a friend from our congregation: *So, Gussie's Sunday school class is doing a short version of* DoveTale. *Gussie was explaining how it goes to Helena. Gussie: "And then Mary is like, 'Who chose me?' And Gabriel says, 'Me and the others and the Boss.'" Helena (incredulously): "Bruce Springsteen?!?" She's five years old. I think my work here is done.* —Jeremy

same position he was in when Gabriel appeared. Gabe then gently takes the baby from the sleepy Joseph, smoothes his hair, whispers, "Marry her Joseph; it's the right thing to do," and exits. A sweet moment I always enjoyed, with eyes closed while Lee leaned in close to whisper. Joseph then wakes with a start and realizes, despite the mysterious bruises, he will indeed marry Mary.

Now, in the 2005 season, during a show in Pennsylvania, Lee and I moved through the familiar paces. The physical pieces went well: I got thrown off the stage to great applause, and was back on the couch, where Lee whispered his line and started offstage . . . without taking the baby. Hence my frantic, "Take it, take it."

What to do? Joseph can't wake up with the baby in his arms. My mind was running through the options. Lee said afterward he thought, *Wow, Ted's really into the role tonight, saying "Take it, take it" in his sleep; he's obviously continuing the inner struggle, as in "Take this from me, I can't do it."* It wasn't till he was completely offstage he realized what I meant.

When Joseph did wake up, I—not so deftly —sort of . . . rolled the baby down my arm and put him down in front of the couch, pretending I hadn't just deposited the coming Lord unceremoniously on the floor, and then, in a stroke of improvisational genius, ignored the bundle lying there.

Stifled laughter

Another favorite memory from a hometown show at EMU's Lehman auditorium:[27]

During the final scene in *DoveTale*, Ingrid and I are seated together as Mary and Joseph, gazing down in adoration at the newborn I am holding in my lap. During the dialogue we both noticed the purple feet of the doll standing in for the infant Jesus. He was upside down.

Hmmm, I thought to myself, *that's unfortunate*. Ingrid, of

---

27 I suppose it's not a mystery we remember the things that go wrong—are we drawn to the tragedy, the conflict, the tension in ways that the smooth, meaningful, seamless performance can never match?

course, noticed and started giggling—it was becoming contagious, and dangerous. Ingrid has a habit of transferring tension into a physical activity, and unbeknownst to her, she began rubbing my thigh—to keep herself from laughing out loud. The more we tried to stop laughing, the harder it became, and the harder she rubbed my thigh . . . the friction began to heat up my leg. I suppose if the show hadn't ended soon, my pants might have caught on fire. She said later she had no recollection of the "fire-starting."

It was in the "arriving at the inn" scene that she started the tradition of seeing how much she could crack me up. After telling me to put the suitcases down so she could sit down . . .

MARY: It feels like it's close. I'm not sure how much more I can take. I thought you said this trip would be three days. Tops.

JOSEPH: Usually it is, however we took rest stops every camel length.

MARY: (*almost about to cry*) I can't help it if I'm retaining fluid.

JOSEPH: I'm sorry, Mary. Don't cry.

MARY: (*Mary is shocked.*) Are you telling me what to do!? I'll cry if I want to.

JOSEPH: Okay, cry. Cry. Don't cry. Whatever you want.

MARY: (*Mary is at the end of her rope—between crying and exploding, like any woman who is about to give birth.*) Fine. You want to keep this marriage together? You want to keep this unit tight? It's three things. It's "Yes, Mary. Right away, Mary. Anything you say, Mary."

JOSEPH: All right.

MARY: Say it!

JOSEPH: Yes, Mary. Right away, Mary. Anything you say, Mary.

(*Mary completely softens.*)

MARY: Give me a kiss.

JOSEPH: Yes, Mary. (*He does.*)

MARY: A hug.

JOSEPH: Right away, Mary. (*Joseph is amused and hugs her.*)

MARY: Now, go knock on that door.

JOSEPH: Anything you say, Mary.

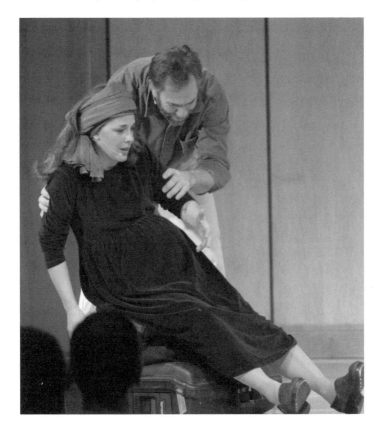

While I was banging on the door of Nigel's inn, Ingrid began sliding off the suitcases, hollering for me to get back and help her—now! I was trying to continue the conversation with Nigel (Lee) while trying to get her back on the suitcases. She would stiffen her body and become a dead weight, purposely making it as difficult as possible. Ingrid is not a big woman, but the position and her refusal to help made it practically impossible to lift her—a madcap slapstick moment. A couple of times I simply slipped and we both collapsed onto the floor, laughing hysterically—which I tried to hide. It became a game for her; just how much could she get me to crack and laugh onstage. One season she was a perfect 11 for 11.

The Not-So-Romantic Life of the Touring Artist

THE ROMANCE OF being a traveling company lasted about two weeks. Life on the road can be tedious. Long drives, many hours simply watching the scenery go by. When people asked us what we did, we would say, "We travel for a living—that's our job. But when we reach our destination, then we get to play."

Being a minor Christian celebrity is an odd thing. Kids come up to you and ask, "Remember me?"

"No, but I'm sure it was a good thing."

What you *want* to say is, "I'm so glad you've been affected by our attempts to create art in a way that honors our integrity. So you've accepted this contract proposal—you, the discerning audience."

But it's hard to make that kind of statement when you're accosted on the sidewalk by fifteen exuberant young people screaming, "Oh my God, it's you, it's them, the guys from this morning—that was awesome!"

A little prestige is something we crave, but on our own terms. The thing is, you don't get to dictate to your audience the terms of just how much recognition you get. That is entirely up to them.

Lest anyone think life on the road is glamorous, consider Canadensis, Pennsylvania, at the same camp where we had first worked together in 1987. Our show was over at ten o'clock at night, and we wanted to go out—something to eat, something to drink. If we were in Los Angeles, Chicago, even Ft. Wayne, the options were many. But we were in Canadensis. We went downtown—nothing open. We went to the next town—nothing open. The next town . . .

There—a Pizza Hut! God bless the Pizza Hut.

The lights were still on, it seemed like a possibility, but no . . . closed!! Closed at ten o'clock. People on the road recognize the "I'm-sure-there's-something-just-over-the-hill" syndrome. If we just go another mile or two . . . all the while getting further and further from the hotel.

But tonight: nothing. Nothing!

Where we ended up?

The BP Mini Market.

Yes, the two guys who slayed the audience earlier, signed autographs, and got a standing ovation . . . we celebrated with microwave burritos and Yoo-Hoo artificially flavored chocolate drink. Ah, showbiz!

Our road van was the Volkswagen Vanagon Sue and I bought from a family at church in 1992. We took out the middle seat and built a lighting box with bars to hang twelve instruments and dimmer packs. We had enough room on the floor of the box for the fifty-pound lighting pole bases, cables, gels, barndoors[28] and other implements of theater that made us feel like we were a real theater company.

The lighting poles slid across the top of the box and rested on the backseat, with an extension that allowed them to reach twelve feet in length. I always thought that if we were in an accident, those poles would slide forward and thrust right through the driver's seat, impaling me and shooting me out through the windshield, like the loser in a jousting tournament.

The van's mileage was undetermined; we never did get the odometer fixed. Plus, the heater was always on, and there was no air-conditioning; we simply disconnected the heater in the spring

---

28 A device for narrowing the beam of a Fresnel, a type of lighting instrument. It is a simple frame with . . . well . . . doors or shutters on it.

of the year, and tried to remember to reconnect it right before winter set in. So in the summer, windows would be wide open.[29]

Since the middle seat was out and the engine was in the rear, if you were seated in the back it felt like an entirely different world and environment. For a number of years we traveled with Cheryl Zook, a lighting and sound tech. During one long trip, Lee took the wheel. I tried to nap in the backseat—back in that distant country. Lee pulled out onto the highway, moving through the gears:

One.

Two.

Three . . . three . . . three . . .

Still in three . . .

Where was four?!?! *He's not shifting . . . Come on, Lee, it's a four-speed, it says so on the knob . . .*

Wind howling through the van, engine screaming right behind me—sixty, sixty-five miles per hour. Now I'm screaming over the sound of the wind, radio, and tortured engine: "Shift! Shift! Shift!"

So much for a nap.

The Vanagon became unreliable to the point where we needed to park on a slope in order to more easily push-start it, on the 73 percent chance it wouldn't start. And the huge dent in the back end (a concrete pole had jumped into my path while I was backing up in a Catholic church parking lot in Cincinnati) helped give it that lived-in look.

Rest areas and scalded penises

It was a typical early morning departure. We stopped in eastern Ohio so we could use the restroom and I could get more coffee. It was my turn to drive. It always seemed a bit counterproductive—the "rest stop, urinal, more coffee" combination. I was sometimes

---

29 Like with so many Vanagons, the back hatch had lost its ability to stay up—faulty hydraulics? At the Fitzgerald Theater in Rockville, Maryland, tech director Lew Dronenberg gave us a stick to prop up the back hatch: six feet five inches tall, light, unobtrusive while stored in the van. The stick became known simply as the "Dronenberg."

tempted to save time by simply dumping the coffee into the urinal.

On this occasion, I needed to use the stall. I got in, locked the door, put my cup on the shelf above the toilet paper dispenser, unhooked my pants, dropped my drawers, and spun around. In doing so, my jacket hooked the coffee cup and pulled it toward my lap, just as I was sitting down. It didn't say "Caution: Coffee Very Hot" on the side of the cup, but it sure should have.

Now my pants were soaked and I was in agony—not to mention out $2.50 for the coffee. I stripped off my shirt, soaked it in cold water, pulled up my pants, and hobbled out to the van, where Lee was moving to the backseat to rest after his driving shift.

"Can you keep driving Lee?"

"Why?"

"I dumped my coffee in my lap."

"Oh . . . you okay?"

"Hard to tell; it hurts too much."

"Did you get your . . . you know . . . ?"

"Direct hit."

"Ouch."

"Yeah."

I was hunched in the back seat, changing pants, socks, trying to alleviate the pain with a wet shirt (which didn't help). We soldiered on after stopping for some minor burn ointment. The show, as they say, must go on.

After the show, having moved through my paces somewhat gingerly, I told Lee, "You were great tonight. I, on the other hand, looked as if I was 'acting with the scalded penis.'" This became a euphemism for various situations:

"What did you think of the play?"

"Okay . . . the female lead was great, but the rest of the cast looked like they were acting with the scalded penis."

That probably meant that they were holding back, not committing to the moment, and protecting themselves with a slightly hunched over demeanor.

"So, you guys are a couple, right?"

In early 2002, Lee and I found out that the leaders of a prominent youth leaders conference thought Lee was a woman, and that we did men and women relationship material. That was part of the reason we weren't hired for the convention: they weren't interested in yet another "relationship duo."

It wasn't the last time we were mistaken for a couple, albeit a different kind of couple. In Austin, Texas, we performed on a Friday night, and were not scheduled to be on again until Sunday morning. That left us with a Saturday evening free in one of the most interesting cities in the U.S.

Lee's cousin Mark Sawin and Mark's wife, Erica, were living in Austin, where Mark was finishing a PhD at the University of Texas. We made arrangements to meet for dinner. We dressed in the best we had—a nice vest combination, with a little flair. Driving through Austin we spotted a jewelry and antique shop called The Silver Armadillo. That being the marsupial of choice for the title of our comedy show, we stopped. While we perused the shop, I noticed several interesting pairs of earrings. I couldn't decide which pair to get as a gift for Sue, and called Lee over to help. The woman behind the counter, after sizing us up, asked me,

"Is this for your sister?"

"I'm sorry?"

"The earrings, are they for your sister?"

"No, they're for my wife."

She laughed at me.

"You're funny."

"No, really, they're for my wife."

"Right."

I gave up. She was positive we—Lee and I—were a couple. She was still chuckling as we left. We weren't even holding hands.

The art of falling down

Falling down is sometimes the best way to get a laugh. As evidenced by a long line of pratfall artists—Jim Carrey, Jerry Lewis,

Bill Irwin, Red Skelton, Buster Keaton, Charlie Chaplin—the fall as an element of surprise is a useful tool in the comedic actor's toolkit. I didn't receive any formal training, but as a decent athlete I could envision the fall and simply replicate what was in my head. (Hey, that's the visualizing exercise I used when I was coaching baseball.)

I suppose I did have some informal training. While in high school, the stairs up to the balcony in our auditorium went up fifteen steps and then took a ninety-degree right turn up another fifteen or so. During lunch periods a number of us would "practice" the most artistic fall from the top level, spilling into view for those watching from the bottom, and then continuing the fall down the remaining steps. Points were allotted for the best surprise to the landing, and the most inventive continuations down the steps. It should come as no surprise that professional wrestling was a great inspiration for many of us.

Of the hundreds of falls I've taken onstage, I've hurt myself only a couple of times, nothing terribly serious. A fully-committed fall can be a great surprise for the audience. It introduces an element

Another early fall onstage.

of danger: someone could get hurt. I especially loved the moment when Lee would throw me off the front of the stage in *DoveTale*. If there was a hardwood floor, we tried to "slide for ten feet on the stomach" before spilling off the stage—hopefully right in front of the first row. Tumbling down steps added another element, coloring the simple fall with a flourish, punctuated with appropriate grunts and other outcries of pain.

One trick is to make sure that the impact of either a dead fall to the ground or of running into a wall is spread out over as much of your body as possible. It's perhaps a rule for a life in the arts: Envision the fall and commit to the action without fear or hesitation, and you just might not get hurt—but there are no guarantees.

Early on Lee and I wrote a sketch included in the original *Fish-Eyes* in which Peter and Andrew are discussing parables of Jesus. The scene, taking off on the parable of the servants who earned equal pay for unequal work, was called "My Dinner with Andrew." It was "playtime" for us, a chance to surprise each other, try to crack each other up. Set in a restaurant, we used the condiments and silverware to illustrate the parable.

Lee's over-the-top absurd frustration with Jesus' enigmatic teaching manifested itself in the indignation of the servants who worked all day:

ANDREW: (*picking up the salt shaker*) Well this really burns my shorts. Do you know how long we've been in your field? Since eight o'clock in the morning with the hot sun beating down on our heads because you're too cheap to provide adequate headgear and we worked all day for you Mr. Boss Man, Mr. Spoonhead, and then this flatware comes traipsing in at the eleventh hour and you want to pay them the same as us! Look at them, the lousy flatware, they're even lying down on the job.

I was straight man to Lee's verbal explosions—when he blew up at the boss man, when he treated the top of the catsup squeeze bottle as a witch's hat and did a great Margaret Hamilton impression as the Wicked Witch of the West, complete with his own soundtrack.

"I'll get you my pretty . . . and your little dog too!"

Then we switched, and I (Peter) made Lee (Andrew) guess which of the seeds I was imitating in the parable of the sower. Starting in a crouch, the seeds would "grow" and then respond to the sun, weeds, or rocky soil. I also performed the seed that fell asleep—"It's not in the story, I just made it up"—the choked seed, the wilted seed, and the fourth seed: the one that was picked up by a bird and carried off . . . into a wall, hopefully to great sound and surprising impact.

Lee would wait for the exquisitely timed response:

"Waiter, can I get some more coffee . . . no, no, none for him, I think he's had enough caffeine."

Before the show, I would scout out the space to find the best wall to run into: was there enough support; were there any protrusions that could injure; could I easily get to the wall from the stage; and again, could I spread out the impact over the entire length of my body?

In 1995, we were in Hillsboro, Kansas, at Tabor College. They had just redone their chapel/theater and were proud of the space. The renovation included a pristine drywalled back to the stage. It was the ideal target: simply turn upstage and run full out into the wall. During the show I gave it a good one, bounced off and fell backwards, and heard a different kind of laughing overlaying the initial laughter.

I glanced at the wall and saw an eight-foot-long crack that started at floor level. I looked over at the students in the front row and winced. They just laughed harder.

Twelve years later Lee and I were back at Tabor—same space. There was now a ceiling-to-floor curtain in front of the wall. I surreptitiously pulled back the curtain, and heard a voice from the balcony:

"It's still there."

The story had been passed down for twelve years, and the crack was left intact as a testament to . . . what? Reckless stagecraft?

Do You Take This Acting Partner, for Better or for Worse, to Have and to Hold . . .?

IN 2003 WE CREATED *The Bob Show*. It wasn't a well-planned artistic decision; however, someone who had hosted two of our previous shows and was looking for a new presentation called and said, "I would book you guys if you had a new show."

To such requests, my first response was usually, "We've been working on a concept; we'll send the contract next week." To which Lee exclaimed, "We have been? A concept? When?!"

And so we wrote *The Bob Show*.

The concept was two actors in final dress rehearsal for a show. The fictional director was Bob, named after our longtime friend Bob Small, and the subtext was Bob as God. In the show the actors wondered why Bob was not showing up, and they argued about the notes that Bob left them, and about who had the proper education to interpret those notes—who, in fact, had a degree in Bobology. Bob never did show up; we just had to work out our differences ourselves. Sort of like God does most of the time.

We hoped the sketches themselves, both biblical and non-biblical, had the clues and directives within them for the actors to find reconciliation; that the lives we are leading are imbued with God's presence, that God will show up in that conflict, in that conversation, in honest living.

The sound person, the unseen character "Darrell," was particularly inept. Sound cues would be the wrong ones or go off at the

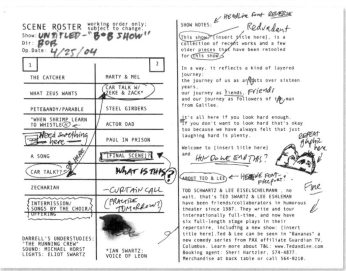

The Bob Show program.

wrong times, helping to build the frustration. On several occasions my son, Eliot, was running sound, and at intermission during one show he heard a boy ask his father why he, Eliot/Darrell, was so bad at his job, and why he still had that job. It was a rather heartless thing to do to our sound guys, when the audience either was too young or didn't have the sophistication to understand that Darrell's ineptitude was part of the show. When our good friend John ran sound, he found himself shrinking behind the furniture when the people would turn and glare at him after yet another misplaced machine gun sound.

Conflict

In *The Bob Show* it was also great fun for Lee and me to portray characters that were pretty much the opposite of our own personalities. Lee, in essence, played me, and I played Lee. Not every audience recognized what we were trying to do, and I wish we'd had a chance to perform it more than seven times.

Our conflicts, like those of most creative partners, were many. I recently found a note in a box of materials from Lee's files. He was a meticulous saver of notes, articles, programs, details of shows, travels, and scribbling. The note was titled, *"THE BOB SHOW"*:

> LEE: Wait a minute! I haven't finished finding out what's
> wrong with your first idea and now you're on to two more!

I don't know if this was a line from *The Bob Show* or if he's just saying what he was thinking about me during the writing process. Either way would make sense, and the passing of time has made it hurt less. A bit.

St. John's Center: near Detroit, February 23, 1997. During a performance, Lee writes in his journal:

> I realize how much I LIKE solitude. In fact, every time I hear a
> door slam in the hall, I fear it is Ted coming to see me. Nothing

against Ted, just that his energies take me in a different direction. Which raises questions like "Do I want to do an Old Testament show/Christmas show/Men and Women's show?" I suppose I do, but only if things will be different with respect to writing. The *Fish-Eyes* thing was hard, I was depressed, etc. Yet, I still think my monologue in F. E., for example, is very powerful. Is that ever acknowledged? I don't want to sorta do Ted's script with Lee on the side. I want the shows to reflect my wisdom too. Generally Ted's instincts are sharp when it comes to stageability and restraint with ideas. I dunno. I just want it to work.

I also prayed a lot regarding youth stuff. Thinking more about this "rock star" stuff. Ted has always been more disdainful and less tolerant, it seems to me, of the exuberance of youth. In fact, it is my conviction that he sometimes fails to let his own children be children. This would be a hindrance, if indeed we want to do Youth Specialties.[30] Do we want Y. S. because of a true call? Or because there is money there—and it would "make" our career. Ted is a driven man, desiring to please Sue, feed the family, etc. I must be sensitive and realistic and understanding of all these things. Maybe I need to get to know Sue better and talk some things out with her, perhaps.

Yes, it was all true. He had articulated the tensions between us, my frustrations about his inability to commit to this career, his frustration with my overbearing hand in ideas and script development. During those times of writing, I would become impatient with his hesitation. If he had brought more ideas, more initiating, would it have worked? Would we have had even more conflict? Battles not around whether to do new ideas, but whose ideas to write or perform?

🙟 🙟 🙟

Lee: "Are we doing a good thing?"
This question came after a show/presentation, during which

---

30 Youth Specialties was a Christian organization whose conferences were great exposure venues. Performing there was usually a nice jump in a career.

I took a question and my answer was, perhaps, not as eloquent as I could have been. I wasn't necessarily as loquacious then as I am now. Trying to communicate the mystery and wonder that I felt was taking place often left me without the proper words, or—worse yet, for Lee—using a word incorrectly. To him, I must have seemed the country boy meat cutter trying to sound intelligent.

We were in Wisconsin at a camp, and *Creation Chronicles* was a very new show. After the show I said, "I think maybe we should look at rewriting the Samuel monologue back into a dialogue."

We had originally created the piece as a scene, and then adapted it to a monologue—in part for expedience—which Lee performed. I had intended to do that monologue in the premiere, but when I took another character, Jeremiah, it made sense to give Samuel to Lee.

Lee took my suggestion to be a criticism of his performance that night. In his mind, I wouldn't want to change a thing if he had been great.

He responded, "Well, you're the god of theater. And by the way, the phrase is 'for all intents and purposes,' not 'for all intensive purposes.'"[31]

It seemed a little childish at the time, but it illustrates an issue that creative teams have when trying to write or create music together. Someone probably needs to be in charge, a head writer, an artistic director, a director. Otherwise we get defensive and petty. I was certainly not immune to that either.

When Lee said that, I abruptly left the room and took the rental car for a very long drive. Once again I felt I was dealing with two entities in the room. One was Lee in all the goodness he possessed, his ability and heart—but the other was the gorilla in the room: his self-image, his depression, his past, his passionless existence. And that infuriated me.

When I came back for the next session, we didn't say anything about the episode and just moved on. Like a couple of good passive-aggressive Mennonites.

---

31 Once again I had mangled the English language in a talk-back session.

On one occasion at home, talking with Sue, my frustrations reached another level:

"That's it!! I'm done! I want to work with an adult!"

"Okay."

"Ingrid and I are going to write a show together and take that on the road!"

"You can't do that."

"Yes we can."

"No—you can't."

"Yes; we've got about thirty minutes of material already written."

(Pause.)

"You can't do that."

I finally saw what she meant—a man and woman traveling together who weren't married or connected wouldn't work for the audiences we were attracting.

"Yes . . . ah . . . that's right . . . I guess I can't do that . . . crap."

Lee was an introvert and perfectionist, whose first reaction to a new idea was why it wouldn't work. Like many perfectionists, he was his own greatest critic. I am an extrovert, addicted to the next fun idea, sometimes to the detriment of the current project. It was our biggest point of conflict.

Lee loved The Beatles, and when we began working and writing together, we decided to use the model Paul McCartney and John Lennon used regarding who got credit for writing. All of our work was delineated "Written by Ted & Lee." It made it easier and less of an ego issue—if someone wrote most of a piece, and the other contributed to the final product, the credit went to both.

Lee referenced the Beatles analogy—and the obvious differences between Lennon and McCartney—often. I found this in his writings following his death. From April 1997:

Ted is clearly Lennon—physical, a bit cynical, terse, pragmatic, fearful of too much praise, but in some ways loves to get on the big art horse. And I, well I'll be taking the role of both McCartney and Harrison in this production.

He was noting the drive he felt I was exhibiting, and his place in that equation—less driven, less harsh, providing a softer edge to the partnership. In the same note, Lee continued to reveal his own anxieties about our relationship and whether it would last:

> I wondered if calling me "bud" meant that he viewed me as a son and not an equal? So this thing about him one day outgrowing his need for me: this is what I fear. Well, we need each other, and when we don't, we'll have something better to do. So stop worrying, ride the boogie, the fact that you make each other laugh is a great sign.

"The fact that you make each other laugh"—yes, that was the glue that ultimately held us together.

Everything but the sex

We often joked that our relationship was evolving into a marriage of sorts. We would on occasion, in public settings say, "It's just like a marriage, without the good stuff." In retrospect that wasn't quite fair, because while we were joking about "everything but the sex," there was a great amount of other "good stuff." Some months we spent a great deal more time with each other than with our wives. It was somewhat inevitable we would write our relationship into a sketch. One of our favorites[32] was entitled "Slow Drift." In it, we addressed the audience from stools, turned slightly away from each other, as if the audience was a private confidant.

LEE: Here's how it happens: bit by bit. It's a slow drift. Like a glacier.

TED: You never think it's going to happen to you.

LEE: It's not like one minute everything is going great and then—bam—suddenly you aren't communicating.

TED: It hurts and you wonder how it all started.

LEE: It's more like rain eroding a hill. You realize one day there's this big channel cut between you, and you wonder why you didn't see it. You know what I mean?

TED: Time was, we could talk and laugh for hours, and NOW I don't even SEE the big picture. It's more like an EXTREME CLOSE-UP of annoyances. You know, if I hear that (*making quotes marks*) "Beatles analogy" one more time I'm gonna scream.

LEE: Take for example Lennon and McCartney.

---

32 So many were "one of our favorites." It's really like trying to choose your favorite child.

TED: That's probably what I'll do.

LEE: When they wrote "Love Me Do" it was two people making each other better. But by the time they did *The White Album* it's like just four individuals. It wasn't really THE Beatles anymore, at all . . . you know what I mean?

TED: You get tired of little phrases like "Do you know what I mean"?

LEE: It's little irritations. Like this "quotes" thing. He thinks it's funny, but it isn't. You know what I mean?

TED: (*a look, a long exhale*) I don't like feeling this way. He just seems so distant now. Like he's not really trying.

LEE: Was it all just blind emotion? I mean, in the early days I thought there was nobody on earth I'd rather write comedy with . . . We could sit in front of the word processor for hours.

TED: You know how you find that one person—the one that's right for you? The one you want to spend the rest of your life writing comedy with.

LEE: But I'm just not getting what I need from him anymore. I hate to admit this, even to myself, but . . . I've been looking at other comedians.

TED: Now, we plan writing meetings and he shows up late or not at all. With the flimsiest excuses.

LEE: I admit it. My eye has wandered. But I don't think I'm the only one. We were at this dinner party not long ago. Duane told this baseball joke and I thought Ted would split a gut. I excused myself and got more punch.

TED: I . . . well . . . there was this other comedian and he seemed to understand. We had a lot in common. Baseball. Kids. You know. And before long we were . . . writing together. You know, at first, just a couple of lines—nothing serious. It was like "why don't you try this" or "this might be funny." I just didn't think anything like that would ever happen to me . . . Before I knew it we had written three sketches and a one-act. It seemed so effortless and easy. Like it was with Lee . . . before . . .

LEE: I was at a Chinese restaurant with Jeremy the other night. We're old friends, so it seemed innocent enough, but still I felt I shouldn't tell Ted where I'd been. So I told him my uncle died.

TED: And what's this pestilence that's been killing all his uncles lately?

LEE: Jeremy makes me feel (*long warm intake of breath*) funny. You know? Like a young comedian. I was doing this bit about the food—this duck entrée—and he was just dying. Oh, man. And then, do you know what he said? He smiled at me and said, "You look like you haven't been laughed at for a long, long time."

🎭 🎭 🎭

When you buy the services of the traveling artist you are paying for the years of perfecting the craft, the writing that might have taken months to finish—plus the travel, the being away from family, the simple drag of road life. We will throw in the show for free. So enjoying your travel companion is paramount. Making each other laugh is a great way to ensure longevity. Lee always— always—could make me laugh. I would like to think he would say the same of me.

One of Lee's gifts was improv. Not classic improv in the stage sense, but finding a nugget in a passing moment and embellishing and polishing that moment until your chest was on fire from laughing.

I'm not sure when Sir Gilbert Hand appeared on the scene. He was not for the general public; perhaps Cheryl Zook, early tech-master who traveled with us during the first years, is the only other person who would recognize one of Lee's darker characters. He was a cross between Sir John Gielgud and Captain Hook, an eccentric English aristocrat with a long-suffering servant, Giles. Their relationship had a healthy dose of sadism with just a hint of homoeroticism. It would start with a question, in a pinched, upper-crust English accent, from Sir Gilbert:

"Tell me Giles . . . how long have you been my manservant?"

That was an invitation to play. I would choose a number at random.

"Forty-six years, sir."

"Forty-six years . . . remarkable . . . how would you fancy a spot of hunting this afternoon, Giles?"

"No, sir, I think not."

"Really, Giles, why is that?"

"You shot me the last time, sir."

"I did?"

"Yes, sir."

"Forty-six years?"

"Yes, sir."

"Remarkable. And in all those years, Giles, have we ever slept together?"

"No, sir, not officially."

"All the pity, Giles, because you seem like a well-set-up young man."

"Thank you, sir."

"Have you been working out?"

"Perhaps a bit, sir."

Sir Gilbert would then continue invitations that always promised violence to Giles.

"Giles . . . would you fancy a game of mumblety-peg[33] then?

"I think not, sir."

"Oh, and why is that?"

"How many fingers am I holding up, sir?"

"Why, three, of course . . . Giles . . . aren't there supposed to be five?"

"Yes, sir, there are."

"Oh, my—perhaps then we should go boar hunting?"

"No, thank you, sir."

"Duck?"

"Lost an eye on that one, sir."

"Well, that explains the patch, then."

"Quite, sir."

"Muskrat?"

And on it would go . . .

---

33 A game of chance involving your spread fingers and a knife thrown to the table.

Finding home on the road

An aspect of life on the road for performers is the sameness of events, combined with the extreme variety of the venues you play in. I sometimes tell college actors that the best physical environment they will ever have for working their craft might be their own campus: here they get the most support, the best theater space, the best lighting and, by the way, the audience can probably walk to your show.

Travel is difficult enough—physically, and sometimes emotionally, draining. Air travel is a huge energy suck. And then you go into a strange environment where you will be asked to create, through an art form that demands relaxation and connection, special moments.

Often I would want to scream at an audience, "Do you people have any idea how hard this is?!! I've been up since four o'clock in the morning; have driven eleven hours; gotten lost twice; I forgot a crucial prop; tried to be grateful, kind, and gracious; worked with your semi-inept sound person on the sound cues—most of which are crucial to the timing necessary for comedy—and now I get to try and be funny!!!"

Most of us performers love what we do. The sacred spaces of the stage pull us out again—out from the comfort of home, from family, seeking again that time of magic when the relationship with the audience is pure and reciprocal. Even now, if I haven't been on stage for a couple of weeks I start to get antsy—it's as if we are addicted to that space in front of people. In a house without an audience, we lose a bit of our sense of self—who am I, why am I here? It's why we put up with travel, creating the task of overcoming obstacles. Life on the road is one large exercise in overcoming.

A number of years ago, as I left home once again, it struck me that my anxiousness about the upcoming performance had nothing to do with the material or my own acting ability. It had everything to do with the unknown of the performance space. Not just whether the sound system would be adequate, or the size of the stage usable, but something deeper.

Actors engage in vulnerability: if you embrace your craft fully, what you reveal onstage is yourself. There is also the tightrope nature of live performance: everyone can see the person on the wire and they instinctively know there is no net. If you stumble, trip, lose your balance, you will fall and perhaps even die—figuratively, of course. That's what makes live theater exciting and different from film: risk.

So the stage is our home. It's where we know the rules, where we can throw our stuff around, spread out, (figuratively) pee in the corners. That stage can be any one of a thousand in the world, but if it has a recognizable configuration—we are here, the audience is there—anything can feel like home. But only after we have walked it, felt it, let it sit in our bodies—then, we're a little safer, and consequently less anxious.

Traveling performers have an interesting and blessed life. We are profoundly grateful for the opportunity to present our art and craft, but the adapting gene or muscle must be highly developed. When someone asks me what I do for a living, I often respond: "Overcome obstacles."

For a long time I have been a huge fan of The Band, a seminal rock band from the '60s and '70s. In 1976 they retired from the road and released a film version of their last concert, *The Last Waltz*. In the film, Robbie Robertson reflects on life on the road: "It's a g** d*** impossible way of life."

Lee and I often used that quote when we'd complete yet another ridiculous eleven-hour road trip in order to set up in forty-five minutes and then make people laugh.

SCENE 11

Adventures with the Actors' Favorite Members of Society: The Audience

WHEN YOU PLAY music for a living you have a safety net: if the audience is difficult, the space too much to overcome, you can pull back to your music, play for yourself. My friends who tour, in bands or solo, talk about this.

When you do theater, you cannot hide: the audience is another character, and if they are not doing their part, or you haven't invited them skillfully enough to join you, it's painful. It has now become work; you reach into the bag of tricks you learned on the road, just to get through. There is no magic in these moments. The holy spirit of art has left the building.

Lee and I tried to hit the mark every time out. There was a level of performance we felt was the bottom line. If we could meet that standard, then we honored the contract, gave the audience their money's worth, and honored the spirit and the craft of the art form. Did we always get there? No. But it wasn't usually from a lack of honest effort.

In fifteen years with Lee, and then five more with various actors, I've missed only two performances. The first was in Kansas, when a snowstorm got us stuck in traffic five miles from home. The other was more memorable: an outdoor festival[34] in Canal Fulton, Ohio. It was mostly a music festival, but the organizers had set up a tent for "theater, magic shows, and storytelling."

This stage had no steps on and off, but someone had placed a cooler there to substitute for steps. It seemed like a logical solution at the time. We were scheduled to do four sets of forty-five minutes each, over two days. The first three went okay. Then, during the break between the third and fourth sets we bought some ice cream, in cones. I walked across the stage and stepped on the cooler, and it tilted forward. The ice cream went up and I did a perfect unintentional pratfall backwards, and my right arm came down on the edge of the stage. I was sure I had broken my forearm.

Lee drove me to the clinic where the X-rays showed no break, just a contusion. I asked if we could perhaps say "severe contusion," since we had missed a show and had made a scene over "I banged my arm."

We never heard from the organizers of the festival—never asked us back, never asked the nature of the injury. Ah, well. Maybe if we were one of those big-name Christian rock bands, singing self-indulgent, smarmy love songs to Jesus, there would have been more concern for my well-being.

Bloomsburg, Pennsylvania. Sunday morning in the park. A good idea, I suppose. Summertime . . . a lovely park down by the river, trees surrounding a large open area. There was a bandstand and stage area, positioned on a low hill.

A grassy knoll—that should have been our first clue.

The audience was to be spread down the gentle slope. The sound tent was about twenty yards out and to our left. When we stepped onstage at eleven o'clock, the sun was nearly overhead, the temperature was in the high 90s (30s, Celsius), and there were

---

34 Outdoor theater means less art and more work. As long as you get paid, that removes some of the pain. You are at an immediate disadvantage: sound will be difficult, silences are never clean, stages are usually too small or inadequate, the distractions are greater, people are less committed, their focus is less defined . . .

Anything else you would like to whine about?

No, I think that's got it.

three hardy souls in lawn chairs forty-five feet away. The rest of the "audience"—the people we had been charged to form a relationship with—was in the shade, literally 110 yards away. More than the length of a football field.

We were doing a mix show, sketches from our biblical story shows, and we usually performed "Song of Solomon" in those sets. Nathan, my character, runs onstage, interrupting Solomon while he is writing the Proverbs:

SOLOMON: A gentle answer turneth aside wrath, but a harsh word stirs up anger. Better a simple dinner of herbs and soup, where love is, than the fatted ox and hatred with it. He who runs with scissors . . . will put his eye out. God helps them that help them— . . . NAAAAAAAH! A fool who returns to his folly is like . . . a dog who returns to his own . . . vomit. I love this. He who keeps in the company of the dull . . .

NATHAN: (*enters carrying a sheet torn from a legal pad*) Solomon! Solomon! You've gotta help me!

SOLOMON: Nathan! I'm writing! Leave me alone.

NATHAN: Listen, you gotta help me. Everyone knows you're good with women.

SOLOMON: Where did you hear that?

NATHAN: It's all over. Everybody knows that. Come on, there's this girl and I'm supposed to talk to her underneath her balcony, and I've got writer's block . . . you've gotta help me.

SOLOMON: Oh very well . . . but tell me something about her. Describe her visage.

Nathan: Her what?

Solomon: Her countenance. (*Nathan still doesn't understand.*) Her face! What does she look like?

NATHAN: Oh, man, she is like really . . . purdy. She's the prettiest girl in all of Jerusalem.

SOLOMON: Yes, yes, Nathan. Aren't they always? I'm talking about specifics.

NATHAN: Specifics?

SOLOMON: Yes, specifics. It's not enough to tell a woman that you love her. You must tell her why. Otherwise, you are as vinegar on the wounds of a sluggard. (*Nathan tries to figure this out.*) Describe her eyes. Use a simile.

NATHAN: A simile?

SOLOMON: A comparison statement using like or as.

NATHAN: Solomon! There she is!

SOLOMON: (*pauses, looks*) She's a Rose of Sharon. A Lily of the Valley. (*He crouches behind Nathan to coach him, à la Cyrano de Bergerac.*)

NATHAN: Yeah, that. Oh my love, how beautiful you are. Your eyes are like . . .

SOLOMON: Doves.

NATHAN: Oh, that's good! Your eyes are like doves. Oh my love, how beautiful you are. Your hair is like . . .

SOLOMON: A flock of goats.

NATHAN: A flock of . . . What?

SOLOMON: A flock of goats.

NATHAN: Goats!? What the—

SOLOMON: Nathan, do you want me to do this?

NATHAN: (*reluctantly nods*) Your hair is like a flock of goats.

SOLOMON: Moving down the slopes of Gilead.

NATHAN: Moving down the slopes of Gilead. My love, how beautiful you are. Your teeth are like . . .

SOLOMON: A flock of shorn ewes.

NATHAN: A flock of shorn ewes.

SOLOMON: All of which bear sons . . .

NATHAN: All of which . . . Is everything gonna be livestock?

During the pivotal scene when Solomon agrees to help Nathan, they move stage right and Nathan "sees" his love on the balcony. Now we are both looking directly at the sun beating down. It has been said that the eyes are the doorway to the soul, and from stage when your eyes reflect your imagination, the audience also sees what is in there. We were, in this case, giving nothing to the audience, because we were now in full squint mode—looking, I'm sure, like a pair of nearsighted old men trying to read the label on a can of evaporated milk. However, since the audience was 110 yards away—except our three brave sunbathing friends on the lawn chairs—it wasn't a huge loss, no one could see our eyes anyway.

I remember looking back at Lee and laughing out loud at the sight of a slit-eyed Solomon, looking quite un-kingly, sweating profusely in his gaudy robe.

We also performed the scene from the Gospel stories, "Feeding of the 5,000," which includes going into the audience to look for food. We were already laughing at the absurdity as we took off for the trees to forage for food from our distant audience. The theatrical magic wasn't going to happen, so we reveled in the ridiculousness of sprinting back to stage, breathing heavily to report in to each other what we had collected, knowing that in three minutes we were going back out to the hinterlands 110 yards away to collect the leftovers.

❡ ❡ ❡

For some reason we were hired to do a junior high assembly in Pennsylvania. It was a public school, so no biblical story. This took away any material we felt could bridge the gap between our ages. Our straight comedy wasn't written for junior high ages, and didn't often translate down. The guy who was so happy to have us there had seen us perform at a conference, and particularly wanted us to do the "Bill in the Booth: Shakespeare Does Basketball" play-by-play. I'm not sure I would have been excited to bring in any form of Shakespeare to a junior high audience, but it was a gig.[35]

Most performers know when they are being set up to fail, and this was starting to feel like one of those times. We were sent to the gym to set up . . .

"The gym?"

"Yes."

"But we passed this great auditorium."

"You're in the gym."

"But, the auditorium—so much more conducive to the relationship between the performer and—"

"Do you want to get paid?"

"Yes."

"You're in the gym."

---

35 *Gig*—where did that word come from? My favorite explanation: when a performer was fortunate enough to secure a paying show he said, "God is good" . . . shortened to *gig*.

So, it was off to the gym, with seating for five hundred on metal bleachers. The "stage" was the middle of the floor, right there on the logo of the school mascot—an angry looking rodent of some kind. Like many gyms, the double set of doors was in the middle of the wall we were facing, the bleachers on either side of those doors.

Which meant there was no one directly in front of us—just five hundred junior highers, house left and house right. We had a fifty-minute set planned. We huddled and decided the motto for the afternoon was "Whatever we do, we can't slow down. No extra pauses, just keep going . . . just keep going . . . *don't slow down* . . . there certainly won't be any laughs to slow us down." It was every bit as bad as we thought it was going to be. Afterward no one talked to us, except the principal. His response?

"Wow, you guys were really punctual."

Our current tagline at the time was "Ted & Lee: Purveyors of fine humor since 1987." For many years after this show, when we would hit our allotted time frame, regardless of the artistic success, we would proudly pronounce to each other, "Ted & Lee: Punctual since 1987."

I was in the locker room afterward, changing and gathering props, when a member of the baseball team came through.

"Hey, you were one of the guys in the show."

"Yeah."

(Pause.)

"You weren't very good."

"That's okay, you weren't either."

❦ ❦ ❦

At a local show in Harrisonburg we were the entertainment for a trucking company, at the country club.

"Well, maybe the food will be good . . . and perhaps they will have a decent space." No. We were not only outside, but our "stage" was set up at one end of the Olympic-sized pool. The audience, of course, was at the other end.

When we got up to perform, Lee said, "This may seem odd to you, but we always insist on having seventy-five feet of water between us and the audience. . . . It keeps the groupies from rushing the stage." Best (and to my recollection, the only) laugh of the night.

Yup. Again, the show was every bit as a bad as we thought.

❢ ❢ ❢

A college in Arkansas. We spent two hours focusing lights and setting cues, and then running a tech rehearsal, reviewing and rehearsing the lighting changes.

Techies are great, but they have a tendency to be . . . overconfident. On this occasion, our guy told us, "We got it."

"Are you sure?"

"Oh, yeah."

"Because we can do this again."

"I got it, piece of cake."

"Okaaaaay."

Within the first five minutes he was off script, one lighting cue ahead. Lee and I not only had to adjust our movements onstage to "find the light," but we had to anticipate the next cue: *So, if this is the light I'm in now—what would be the lighting for the scene, not the next one, but the one after that, because that's the one he's on.*

He knew something was wrong, but he couldn't adjust it on the fly.

After the show we vowed to never again put the show in the hands of the tech crew. So the next time we encountered an enthusiastic lighting tech:

"We got a full lighting system . . ."

"That's great. Just give us a full warm wash."

". . . with a new dimmer system."

"Nice. But just the wash, a combination of ambers and blues."

"I've run the last three productions here."

"Good for you. Just . . . the warm . . . wash. . . . Please."

SCENE 12

The Artist:
Selfishness and Selflessness

A LIFE IN THE ARTS is not quite a humanitarian's life. It's not really a life of service, in the way we think about mission work, social work, or teaching. It is, however, an intriguing and continually fascinating balance of selfishness and selflessness, constantly thinking and observing how an action, a vision can fit into what we write, paint, sculpt, or create.

Acting is a balance between narcissism and ego. And complete vulnerability. Believable acting rips away the shells we all carry to reveal ourselves—without ever forgetting where we are, what we are doing, and how the audience is reacting. It can seem as if performers are constantly looking at themselves, judging reactions, looking inward. Artists, however, should be looking outward, using the raw material at hand—themselves—to express something larger than themselves.

When you work so hard to become known as artists, marketing looms large. For the two of us Mennonite guys, it was a necessary part of the business, regardless of how it felt. And we certainly felt conflicted: the idea of blowing our own horn was close to the sin of pride, which was just around the corner from even worse sins for Mennonites—like drinking, swearing, dancing, or an evening that included all three. A prideful, cursing, drunken dancer—that about covers all of the sins, I think.

A director friend, Tom Arthur, asked me,

"Why are you practically running offstage after the show is over? They're applauding for you."

"I know that."

"If you rush offstage in a fit of Mennonite angst brought on by this odd sense of humility, these people will be obliged to stop applauding or feel stupid for appreciating the show so much."

"Right."

"You can't do that."

"Got it."

"You are punishing your audience for applauding."

"That's not what I . . . I'm sorry."

"And stop apologizing."

"Right . . . sorry."

"Jesus Christ."

Blowing our horn for marketing purposes meant we needed a brand. A brand isn't just a name, it becomes an identity. It's what market trust is connected to. In our case, a particular style of comedy and theater morphed into a brand: Ted & Lee—each of our names, separated by the ampersand. There was a simple symmetry to it—three letters each.

This brand made us feel inseparable before our audiences, without individual identities. If one half of a brand either dies or leaves, it sounds peculiar: Sears Roebuck became Sears—you got used to it after a while. Rowan and Martin, Laurel and Hardy, Abbott and Costello were never anything except the two of them together.

Andrew, the son of good friends, was in second grade when he inadvertently verbalized what real branding sounds like. His school bus would come around the circle at Waterman Elementary and drop him off. Lee's wife Reagan was dropping their kids off one morning, and the bus cut the corner a little tight, creating a bit of a fender bender between Reagan's van and the bus. There was no real damage done, but it was exciting for the kids on the bus. That night when Andrew got home, he told his mother excitedly,

"Mom, Mom, today AndLee's van hit our bus!"

Audiences: can't live without 'em, can't live with 'em

There is a relationship that most performers find sacred: the relationship between the audience and the performers themselves. There are some directors, actors, and other performers who feel that if no one is offended, they have not done their job. Others feel *everyone* needs to be offended. Lee and I didn't believe this to be true. However, it is sometimes reassuring to know that the work we are doing could possibly be distressing to some. Art should entertain and inspire, but also make you feel uncomfortable—on occasion.

When we started combining comedy writing and biblical story, we assumed we would get a lot of negative feedback. The mostly open responses to our odd interpretations constantly surprised us. Ralph MacPhail Jr., theater professor at Bridgewater College, once noted: "It helps that you—the disciples—are the densest ones in the room. Everyone else is smarter. This makes them feel good about themselves and better able to accept a different or stretching interpretation."

Not everyone was happy though, especially when we began messing with people's images of God and, to our great surprise, angels. In a September 17, 1998, letter to a church publication, R.M. of Mount Joy, Pennsylvania, wrote:

> Regarding Ted & Lee taking a crack at the Old Testament. I find it repulsive and obnoxious to see the holy God of the Bible reduced to someone who could be acted out in a play. What has Mennonite-ism come to? If Menno Simons were to return from the grave he would surely put the Mennonite church in the same category as he did the Catholic church in his day. God help us and deliver us from such ungodly influences!

I'm especially fond of the exclamation point.

These next two comments came after the same show, same performance, same denomination, same gender:

"If you had been born for no other reason than this show, that would have been enough." —C.N.

"Please refund my money for the play Monday night. It is heresy and you should be ashamed of belittling God like that period and to call man God!? I will be more than happy to converse with you about this." —T. P.

Interesting.

The last man left his address and so I sent him his money back with a note and an additional twenty dollars, telling him to take an artist out to lunch. Never heard from him. One would hope he has grown outward instead of inward.

Another favorite:

It is with much reluctance and after careful thought that I'm sending you this letter regarding the fund-raising banquet of September 18. My wife and I had a great deal of difficulty with Ted and Lee's comic presentation of the Creation Chronicles. In fact, words are not sufficient to express our utter dismay at the way they portrayed God and Michael.[36]

And another:

We could not believe our ears and eyes as they made the events of creation and other scenes look funny. It is as if they were downgrading the sovereign God to a humanized God saying things like "I don't know," etc. When it came to Michael's encounter with Abraham telling him about circumcision we were aghast. Is this the way it really happened? And if not, why are they presenting it this way? What is our goal? To reach people through this kind of humor? We shuddered when it came to Solomon's description of the bride. We were utterly afraid they would go on to describe details of her body. I heard some Bible teachers describe Song

---

36 When they don't get details right, it lessens the sting a little—pretty sure we say Gabriel a lot, and never mention Michael.

of Solomon as epitomizing the intimate love and holy relation between the Bridegroom and his Bride.[37]

Later, when we performed that show and I was playing God, Lee would introduce it this way: "While Ted will be portraying a form of God, we are in no way limiting God to the attributes of Ted." That usually got a laugh, and maybe softened the way for those seeing God portrayed onstage as somehow distressful.

---

37 One of my favorite lines in the entire Song of Solomon scene is the final line: "I do believe this is the most beautiful love song I have ever written—I just hope it's never taken out of context." I guess he didn't get that line.

SCENE 13

What Are You Doing Here?

IN 2004 I WAS in a local production of Warren Leight's *Glimmer, Glimmer and Shine*, directed by my old friend Tom Arthur. I told him I was anxious to be in a show I didn't write, directed by an outside perspective. "I want to see if I'm getting better, or just getting a bigger bag of tricks," I said.

His answer: "What's the difference?"

"Ah, I'm not sure."

"Neither am I."

"Okay."

I was playing Marty Glimmer, a trombone-playing heroin addict who played in the big bands that toured in the '50s. Dying and estranged from his brother, who gave up the horn to go into business, Glimmer reconnects with, not his brother, but his niece, his brother's daughter.

I had a ball. I lost weight to appear gaunt; I would shave on Sunday night and then didn't the rest of the week in preparation for the weekend shows. On show nights I would wake up in the morning, wet my hair, and not touch it after that. I did all the fun, cool things actors get to do. I didn't need to worry about production issues, marketing, travel, lights, sound—anything except being the best actor I could be. I even enjoyed the matinee when only four people showed up. We gave those hardy four a good show.

After a performance a young man approached me.

"What are you doing here?"

"I'm not sure I know what you mean."

"In Harrisonburg, why are you still in Harrisonburg? You should be in L.A. or New York."

Ah, I see. It was a compliment. I said, "Maybe I could have done that, but I really like who our sons are becoming and that might not have happened if we had moved. I might not have liked who I might have become."

Sometimes I do wonder. Tom, while I was in class with him, assumed if you have the ability, you have an obligation to try and take it as far as you can. What is the responsibility? Did I owe it to ... art? God-given gifts? Did I shoot as high as I should have? Was I doing just what I was supposed to, and no more?

When a professor from Marshall College adjudicated *The Foreigner* while I was in college, he gestured to me and asked director Barbra Graber, "What's he going to do?"

"He's going to seminary."

"Really? What a waste."

What a wonderful juxtaposition to folks back home—my seminary sponsors—thinking, "He's acting. What a waste."

Harrisonburg was a little pond. The Christian theater arena is also a little pond, and the Mennonite pond even smaller. Perhaps part of the reason Lee and I were successful was because in the world of "church drama," the bar is pretty low. In fact Lee and I rebelled at the phrase *church drama*—much the same way we despised the word *skit*. In fact we wrote a litany around the issues of "church drama":

TED: Good morning, I'm Ted.

LEE: And I'm Lee.

TED: We are actors and writers of theater who create much, but not all, of our work in the church.

LEE: Sometimes when people hear this they conclude that we therefore perform

BOTH: church drama.

TED: And they run for the door screaming

LEE: before we've even started.

TED: Why is this? We think it's because people have never actually experienced the art of theater at church.

LEE: They have only seen

BOTH: church drama,

TED: or perhaps choric readings,

BOTH: like this.

LEE: In a moment Ted and I will perform a theater piece called *The Last Supper*.

TED: We don't consider it to be church drama. So, what's the difference?

LEE: It's the difference . . .

between a straight line and a spiral;

between giving answers and asking questions;

between an interest and the passion;

between control and risk.

TED: Between the arrogance of knowing and the humility of mystery.

Between *American Idol* and *Aretha Franklin*.

Between summer camp and six years at Second City in Chicago.

LEE: Church drama too often asks us what we already know and not what we don't. It's the difference . . .

between sermon and story.

Between propaganda and art.

TED: Theater should make you feel like new sneakers. Theater is color, wonder, and the unexpected. It is saying less . . .

. . . saying less

. . . saying less

. . . saying nothing.

LEE: It is the magical, mystical, and the rightness of threes.

It is the laughter of recognition.

It is the laughter of the light.

It is the laughter of surprise.

I suppose I will always wonder a little bit about the "highest calling." The pull to try your craft at the highest level—it's still there.

SCENE 14

Negotiating the Real Marriages

FOLLOWING LEE'S TIME at the treatment center in Maryland, on the day he moved back to Harrisonburg, he met a lovely woman who was moving into the townhouse next door. He thought she was angry; she thought he was terribly full of himself. They became friends and overcame those first impressions to fall in love.

Lee and Reagan were married in 1998—a beautiful outdoor wedding that Sue and I participated in. I wrote a message, and Sue and I read a retrospective of Lee and bride Reagan's relationship using only lines from our plays.

There was a strong correlation between Lee's commitment to Reagan and her kids and a commitment to career and business. We were finding equilibrium.

We both now had responsibilities to someone "back home."

Good friend and actor Curt Cloninger tells of the time when his wife cut off a "conversation" with this rejoinder: "No one is applauding here."

What she meant was, "You are no longer onstage; that other world of ninety-minute pseudo-intimate relationships with hundreds of people is over. Welcome back to the real world. Now it's your turn to make dinner, bathe the kids, clean the house, and the lawn's been calling your name for five days. I'm off the clock."

We traveling artists with families know we live in two worlds, and those worlds don't always overlap. It can be a wrenching thing

to come off the road, where you are acclaimed and fêted, and experience the reentry of mundane tasks and conflicts: the lawn, the diapers, the house that needs cleaning, the spouse who couldn't care less about the people you met and the fun you had. Balancing the public persona and the private one is delicate. You cannot fall into the habit of believing in your own public persona, because—believe me—your wife sure doesn't.

Sometimes we would feel sheepish about the experiences we had, so we would downplay the scenery or location. "Yeah, the hotel . . . not so great . . . no fun people . . . terrible experience . . ." It's not a good idea to have too much fun on the road.

When we travel, we feel a focus shift, whereby the most important people in the universe are changing from your family to the people who are coming to see you. And women seem to be really good at noticing when the shift begins—go figure. Sue has often said there is a day before the trip when I check out—reviewing props lists, packing the suitcase,[38] beginning the anxiety of a new space. And the day after the trip, usually exhausted, jazzed from

---

38 I'm an over-packer—especially traveling by van. If you think you *might* need it, read it, wear it, fix it, by all means throw it in the van.

the energy of hundreds, sometimes thousands, of people—often completely drained—not wanting to talk to anyone.

Without the understanding of those who stay home, the kids who put up with absences, the wife who soldiers on—this life would be impossible.

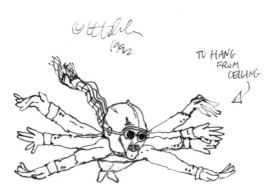

TO HANG
FROM
CEILING

SCENE 15

Ted & Lee:
Reaching Cruising Altitude

FROM 2001 TO 2007, Lee and I had reached a consistent
level of income: between $50,000 and $60,000 each; pretty good
for actors living in the theater non-mecca of Harrisonburg. We
had a line of videos, posters, and T-shirts. We had acted in forty
different states, Canada, Japan, and Africa, and our scripts were
sold and produced all over the world. We had created a business
and careers out of nothing, had developed a new style of comedy.

During one trip, we stood together on a cliff overlooking the
Oregon coast to our left, the impossibly green hills of Douglas fir
and redwoods to our right, the sun reflecting off the Pacific Ocean.
We had stopped because it was a long drive, and we had drunk too
much coffee. As we reflected in admiration and relief, Lee said,

"It is our humor—what has brought us here. Today."

And it was. We knew if we weren't funny, we wouldn't be on
the coast of Oregon, or in Nairobi, Kenya, or in any one of the
wonderful towns across this continent.

My congregation back home in Lansdale, Pennsylvania, had
come to peace with the direction of my "calling." One of the prin-
ciple contributors had stated publically, "It was the best investment we ever made."

We had a contract with Abingdon Press, the publishing arm of
the United Methodist Church. In the fall of 2006 they had asked
us to produce thirty-two new video episodes for a curriculum. This

was a huge undertaking for us, but was also the "big shot" at getting product filmed and produced to sell for the next five to ten years, with the largest potential market we had ever had. It was to be our retirement income—this influx would be money on top of regular tour income.

Lee's son, Gabe, born in 2002, was a source of wonder and love for Lee. Our oldest son, Eliot, was married. As I turned fifty, things were looking bright. The career path seemed to be making sense. We had seen much of the United States, met an amazing group of creative and inspirational people. I was healthy, Sue and I were doing well, the boys had grown up happy and strong . . .

What could go wrong?

Act 3

Climax

Wherein the play comes to a turning point, a change for better or worse, in the journey of the protagonist. If the story is a comedy, events which to this point have gone badly, will begin to look up. If the story is a tragedy, the opposite will happen . . .

Is this story a tragedy or a comedy?

MISSPELLING IS
INTENTIONAL—
WILL BE
PART OF
SHOW.

SCENE 1

The Comedy Dies

It WAS THURSDAY, May 17, 2007. Making supper, I had just put the pork chops on the grill, when the phone rang. It was Carmen, a friend, but not someone I expected to call.

"Hello."

"Hello, Ted. It's Carmen."

"Hi."

"Is someone with you?"

It's never a good sign when someone asks you that.

"Yes. Why?"

"I'm at Lee and Reagan's—you need to come over."

"Why?"

"It's Lee. You need to come over. . . . It's bad."

That's all she said. I started to get an odd feeling, like being inside a movie. When your mind is shoved into an unfamiliar place, a place it's never been before, sometimes the body remembers how to go about tasks . . .

turning the grill off . . .

putting shoes on . . .

finding the keys to the car.

I pulled the chops off the grill, told our boarding student where we were going, and Sue and I drove the mile or so over to the Eshlemans', neither of us saying a word, afraid that if we talked about our fears at that moment, they would turn out to be true.

We pulled up out front and, seeing nothing amiss, walked in the front door, which was standing open. No one there. There was an eerie, strange calmness. We walked through the house downstairs—still nothing—until we went out the back door downstairs, and saw the police and paramedics.

Carmen met us at the gate in the fence.

"We lost him" was all she said.

Between 3:00 and 4:30 in the afternoon, Lee had ended his twenty-year struggle with depression by taking his own life. The clichés are true; it didn't seem real. I had the bizarre feeling I was inside a play I was writing. All of my responses to the police questions felt scripted:

When did I last see him?

What were we doing?

What was his state?

We had spent four hours together that day, doing the business we had done thousands of times. We had set up for a show: placing the props, spiking the set pieces, running lines, ironing costumes— the rituals of actors. I knew he was not doing well emotionally. At one point he called Reagan and I heard him say, "I'm trying. I'm singing."

We set up for the show *Live at Jacob's Ladder*, a play with music we had written together with Ken Medema, directed and dramaturged by our old friend Bob Small. Jeff Raught had stepped in for Ken and recreated his role. We were ready for the big marketing push for this show. It was our next big offering as a company, our sixth full-length show, and it had taken a lot of our attention in the previous six months. We loved the show. We believed Lee had done his best design work on the promotional materials.

Jacob's Ladder is from the book of Genesis: the story of two brothers, Jacob and Esau, twin sons of Isaac and Rebecca. Jacob steals the birthright and blessing from his brother Esau and runs for his life. After twenty years he attempts to return home, but he is still afraid of the wrath of Esau. And so he sends ahead gifts of cattle, donkeys, sheep, and goats. The pivotal returning scene at the end of the play includes this dialogue:

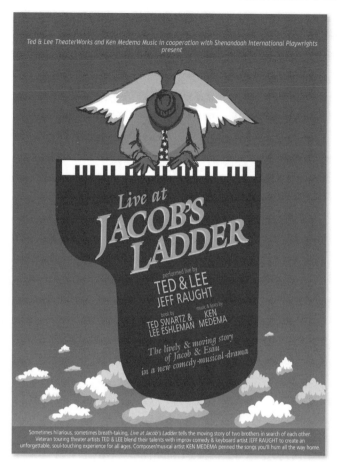

JACOB: I can explain . . .

ESAU: No you can't. You stole my birthright and my blessing. Those were mine. Papa wanted me to have them.

JACOB: I know what I did.

ESAU: And now you want to come home.

JACOB: Yes.

ESAU: Just like that.

JACOB: No, not just like that—I brought you
enough to satisfy anyone. Do you know what
this represents?

ESAU: I don't want your sheep, I don't want
your camels, your donkeys, your goats. I've
got all I need. With or without bows!

JACOB: All right! What do you want Esau?

ESAU: I had a brother once.

JACOB: So did I . . .

The scene continues until Jacob does ask for forgiveness. Esau
(Lee) in response spits into his hand, like they used to do when
they were kids, and holds it out to Jacob. While Jeff sings Ken's
haunting "Healing of the Heart," Jacob spits into his own hand
and takes Esau's hand—and the brothers embrace.

Another play, another brothers story, another embrace to end
a play.

Four days earlier we were in Grand Rapids, Michigan, for a
Sunday morning show. We performed two sets of a shortened version of *Fish-Eyes*, pieces we had performed well over a thousand
times. The first set was a little rough, not up to the standard we set
for ourselves—we both were tired, the audience was sluggish, Lee
seemed distracted. We knew it wasn't our best work; we reviewed
the scenes again and vowed between services to improve it. The
second service went much better. The response was very positive,
and we finished with the final lines from the show, when the disciples Peter (me) and Andrew (Lee) realize the identity of the mysterious man who has been hollering at them:

PETER: Andy, who's that on the shore?

ANDREW: I don't know. But he's hollering at
us.

BOTH: WHAAAAAAAAAAAT!!!!!!!!????????

PETER: Have we caught anything?

ANDREW: Oh, ha ha ha. Aren't you the funny one, you halibut heckler.

BOTH: NOOOOOOO!

(*They turn away, then hear the call again.*)

BOTH: WHAAAAAAAAAT?

ANDREW: Caaaaa . . .Caaa . . . Cashew. Nuts. Cashew nuts. Cashew nuts on the other side. Cashew nuts?

PETER: Cashew nuts?

ANDREW: Did you bring a snack?

PETER: No, I didn't bring one.

BOTH: WHAAAAAAAAAAAAT?!

ANDREW: Caaaa . . . Caaaaa . . .

PETER: Here he goes again. . . .

ANDREW: CAST! Okay, second word. (*gives a charades symbol*) You . . . you . . . your . . .

PETER: He's talking about us.

ANDREW: Cast your . . .

PETER: What do you cast?

ANDREW: Nets! Cast your nets! Cast your nets on the other side. That makes a lot more sense than cashew nuts.

BOTH: (*pause*) WHHHHYYYYY?! (*can't hear the answer*) WHAAAAAAAT?

PETER: Andy, he's not projecting at all.

ANDREW: There is no diaphragm support. Cast
your nets on the other side. Thank you!
Thanks for that great advice.

(*Andrew turns away, while Peter watches for a
short time.*)

PETER: Hey Andy, why don't we just do what he
says?

ANDREW: (*laughing*) Give me one good reason.

PETER: I don't think he's gonna shut up until
we do.

ANDREW: (*looks out at the figure on shore,
considers*) Okay. But Pete, let's really try
and get this one out there. (*They gather the
net and cast in rhythm, on the other side.*)
Well I hope he's happy . . . (*Peter looks at
Jesus as if to say, "How's that?" Suddenly,
they are pulled rapidly to the side; hang-
ing off the edge of the stage/boat.*) I think
we've got something.

PETER: Oh, do you think so? (*They pull
in, three times, then see a huge catch.*)
WHOOOOOOO! Would you look at all the fish!

ANDREW: Holy mackerel!

PETER: I have never seen so many fish in one
catch, there must be a hundred and . . .

ANDREW: . . . fifty three. One hundred and
fifty-three in a single cast. Man, we've still
got it!

PETER: It is a good thing that we decided to
cast on this side of the . . .

ANDREW: 'Cause we said, it's not happening
over here, so we said we would cast . . .

(*They stop, then look to the shore.*)

PETER: Who IS that?

ANDREW: I don't know, but he's cooking something.

PETER: What's he making?

(*They sniff.*)

ANDREW: Fish.

PETER: And bread.

ANDREW: Huh. Fish and . . . (*They suddenly
realize who it is on the shore, and begin
laughing.*) Bread and fish. Peter, do you think
there will be enough?

(*They both laugh, then embrace.*)

I had no idea the last words we would ever speak on stage
together would be "Do you think there will be enough?" While we
had written the line to reflect the real question as a joke—in reference to Jesus' ability to create an abundance of food—it also can
mean "enough love?" "enough answers?" "enough time?" "enough
_____?"

The answer that rang in my head the weekend of the funeral
was "No, I guess not."

In the scene, as the brothers realize their lives will continue to
be affected by Jesus, they laugh and embrace.

The last physical act we performed together on stage was a hug.

Pushing too hard?

After we set up the *Jacob's Ladder* show the morning of Lee's death,
we ordered out for lunch and went across the street to my house
to eat. It wasn't until hours later that I noticed he never touched
his salad.

That same morning Reagan had suggested we look at the year in pieces, so Lee brought large sheets of white paper and he drew calendars on them—May through November. We had been contracted to write and produce a new show to premier in a month and a half, early July, and our video project with Abingdon Press was looming. It was also going to be the busiest touring summer we ever had: six multiple-day conventions in addition to regular touring, plus finishing the production for a new *DoveTale* DVD. It was a ridiculous schedule, and I felt a certain amount of guilt for pushing Lee as I was—or as I thought I was.

It was a twenty-year theme with us: I would push to do all we could, and Lee would resist. Years before, we were interviewed separately for a local TV special, and the interviewer asked, "What do you like best about each other *and* what do you like least?"

Lee's response to the least: "I wish he wouldn't keep driving us to what's next."

My response: "I wish he would take more chances."

Those were the questions used in the interview. I wish she had included what we liked best about each other:

Lee: "His passion."

Ted: "His heart."

The one resisting the impulse to always be creating and dreaming can be cast in a negative light, when in reality perhaps that caution is a necessary part of a healthy relationship. Lee acted as a governor on my impulsive dreams. When we premiered *The Bob Show*, I was sitting on the edge of the stage at a break in our dress rehearsal. Lee looked at me and said, "You're thinking about the next show aren't you?"

I sheepishly nodded and he rolled his eyes and walked away.

Perhaps I abused his remarkable talent to recognize the humor in a script, to make it better, and especially to learn quickly. We were always learning the scripts at the last minute, always underrehearsed—walking the thin line between flying and falling. I had struggled for years to discern why I found most projects underrehearsed.

Maybe it has something to do with my persistent fear that the writing isn't good enough, and that I must count on myself and other talented performers I've worked with to make the material work. The audience then becomes the de facto director. If the moment, pratfall, or line gets a laugh, then it works.

I really don't mind rehearsals—for work I haven't written.

Perhaps rehearsing reminded me of our initial writings and the conflicts we had to overcome. We were naive about the process of writing together. Initially it seemed like play, and perhaps we thought it would always seem so. When it became work, ego and resentment cropped up. Early writing often happened in my office, on my Apple II clone. Lee found my fumbling at typing excruciating, so he often took over that task. Now, if you are throwing out ideas, expecting the typist to automatically record all your magical musings, and he doesn't—he has acted as de facto editor. So we would, despite my poking at the keyboard, share that task.

Lee's early writing for stage tended to be witty, lengthy, monologue-ridden opuses. So the editing process often meant taking away words, which young writers can easily interpret as a negative.

My writing was sparse, underwritten and minimalist, with emphasis on action and image, sometimes just a concept scribbled on scrap paper.

Lee would look at it, pause, and say, "Will I get some lines?"

Then we would often add words, build the sketch line by line— a positive energy of adding to, rather than taking away. Once Lee understood what I was attempting in the sketch or scene, then he would lend his creative brilliance to add lines, add movements, bring in a nugget that would allow the piece to really fly. Later, as we grew as writers, we learned to better navigate this necessary part of the creative process.

❦ ❦ ❦

Lee was very anxious about the fall schedule, so we broke the months down: when the production team would need to be contracted, when the new writing would get done, when rehearsals would happen, when sets would be built, where the money was coming from—and when that pesky new show premiering in six weeks would get put up.[39]

Lee was understandably concerned about how all of this would get done. I tried to reassure him that we could do it—we always did, including the month several years earlier when we premiered two shows—and promised him again that I would stop doing this to him.

He probably didn't believe me.

He said, almost offhandedly, "The new show for July will be fine. I know you will write the rest of the show in the next two weeks and we'll finish the rehearsals in June. We'll be tweaking up until the day before and it'll be fine, but . . ." He was mostly concerned about the video shoots.

At 2:10 we broke and I went across the street to help Sue teach an acting class at the high school. Lee scribbled a few notes on the contract proposal for Abingdon Press and left the house, his familiar artistic scrawl crawling down the side of the page. I don't remember if we said goodbye.

At 4:00 I met with Eliot, our oldest son, to review the lighting cues; he was running the board that night.

At 4:15 I called Lee's cell phone to clarify a cue point. He didn't answer. Days later when I listened to the messages on his phone, it was eerie to hear my voice, trying to be cheerful for him, oblivious to what was happening right then.

I don't remember if we said goodbye.

¶ ¶ ¶

---

39 "Put up a show" is a quaint saying. Always reminds me of canning fruits and vegetables during the harvest season: you "put up" pears, or peaches. Must be a Pennsylvania thing. You can also "mount" a show—I guess like a horse.

Many of us have a common problem of mixing up our kids' names. In fact, I'm pretty sure my grandfather never called me Ted directly. It was always RobertSamuelTimTed—from my Dad, to Dad's first cousin, to my brother, to me. So, fourth in line. It must have been exhausting to always use four names when one would do just fine. I never had too much trouble with our three boys. However, I was constantly exchanging Tim, my brother, with Lee and then Lee with Eliot, our oldest son. I never used the younger boys' names for Lee. I'm not sure why. But I would regularly exchange Lee for Eliot and vice versa.

Standing in the Eshlemans' backyard that dark day, the one person I realized I couldn't talk to was Eliot. To this day, I'm not sure why. I left that up to Sue, who I knew would be strong enough, much in the same way she was the only one who could deliver the "sermon" when we buried Shemp, the beloved family dog. Shemp, the fourth Stooge, because we already had "The Three Stooges," Eliot, Ian, and Derek.

I did call John, a mutual friend. The day before, the three of us had attended a Todd Snider concert in Washington D.C. We left at four o'clock in the afternoon, had dinner at the club, and enjoyed two acts: Todd, and opening act, Dan Bern.

On the way up, Lee drove; he handed me the mail from the P.O. box. I opened some correspondence from an insurance agent, responding to my inquiring about business-partner insurance. I read how, in case of the illness or death of one of us, the policy would keep the other partner from losing income. We laughed because my policy was more expensive than Lee's, since he was younger and consequently less of a risk.

We never had a chance to buy it.

That evening, we had a great time. Lee seemed to be in good spirits. We enjoyed Todd, but probably enjoyed Dan Bern more, especially a haunting song entitled, "God Said No." We bought the CD and played it through on the way home. Lee slept most of the way; John and I talked about baseball. The CD stayed in the van's player.

I met God on the edge of town
Where the wind meets the stillness
Where the darkness meets the light
Where the ocean meets the sky
Where the desert meets the rain
Where the earth meets the heavens
On the edge of town I met God

I asked God
Do one thing for me
Send me back in time
Send me to Seattle
Let me go
Find Kurt Cobain
Take away his gun
Take away his bullets
Talk to him
Make him wanna live
Tell him how we love him
Help him see his glory
God Said No
If I sent you back
If you really found him
You would only ask him
If he could
Help you get a deal
If he knows a lawyer
If he can help you
God Said No

I asked God
Do one thing for me
Send me back in time
Send me to Berlin
Let me find
The one they call Hitler
I will stalk him

I will bring him down
I will bring along
A powerful gun
Loaded with bullets
Obliterate his memory
God Said No
If I sent you back
You would get caught up
In theory and discussion
You would let your fears
Delay and distract you
You would make friends
You would take a lover
God Said No

I asked God
Do one thing for me
Send me back in time
Send me to Jerusalem
Let me go
Let me go find Jesus
Let me save his life
As they try to kill him
Let me take him down
Down from the cross
Take the iron from his body
Try to heal his wounds
God Said No
If I let you go
If you really found him
Walking with the cross
You would stare
Your tongue no longer working
Eyes no longer seeing
Ears no longer hearing
God said Time
Time belongs to me

Time's my secret weapon
My final advantage
God turned away
From the edge of town
I knew I was beaten
And that now was all I had
God Said No[40]

Songs, tears, memories, and laughter

Lee had dropped a grenade into so many lives; for many, even now years later, it's a seminal moment. Where were you when you heard?

Thursday night, the night of his death. A group of us met at Community Mennonite Church—family and close friends, members of the pastoral team. Members of our small group from church came to the house after we got home. Church was to become central for us over the next couple of days.

Friday morning, after a sleepless night for both Sue and me, I went to the coffee shop across the field to help plan the chapel program to replace the one Lee and I were to perform that morning at Eastern Mennonite High School. When I started the van, the CD was still in the player, and I heard Dan Bern's song, "God Said No."

I sat and cried again, thinking that despite the pleas of Lee, God said no.

Or did God say yes?

I still don't know.

There was a candlelight service Friday night at Community Mennonite Church. Sue and I sat up front. People would come forward, light a candle, say a prayer, come over to Sue and me. We decided to stay the entire evening; people seemed to want someone to express their grief to physically. To hold, hug, touch, or just see.

---

40 Dan Bern, "God Said No," Kababa Music (ASCAP). Used by permission.

One longtime friend, Jerry Holsopple, came that evening. He had been the director and producer of *Fish-Eyes*, the video curriculum series that Lee and I had done in 1994. Lee and I had written the stage show and the video series at the same time that winter and spring. In one of the scenes, Peter gives Andrew, his brother, a hard time because Andrew always seemed to follow the latest trend in hot new messiahs. Peter then asks Andrew why this Jesus was going to be any different than, for instance, Reginald the Anointed, messiah wannabe. Lee had designed pamphlets from Reginald the Anointed, and when the brothers caught a huge catch of fish later in the scene—because they had followed Jesus' directive to go back out and throw some more net—the extra fish were wrapped in pamphlets of Reginald the Anointed. This was one of Lee's great gifts: creating memorable works of art, disguised as props.

When Jerry came up that night, he lit a candle and came over to Sue and me. As we hugged, he whispered in my ear:

"I had a visitor last night . . . Reginald the Anointed."

I laughed harder than I had in days, and I can still hear the solitary sound of my laughter in that silent space of mourning.

I said, "There is only one other person in the world who would find that as funny as I do, and he's not here."

That night I asked Jeff if he would just "sing the songs from the show." I wanted to hear the music from *Jacob's Ladder* one last time. I announced at the service that we would be doing that. Around fifty people showed up, and Jeff began the "concert." When it came to a part that was a duet with Lee, Jeff asked me to come up, and I sang Lee's part—in essence, doing my best imitation of Lee singing Laban's role. It felt like the right thing to do. It was the beginning of a unique healing experience through the arts: performing and writing my way out of grief.

Later that night Nate and Elaine and Alden and Louise, two couples from our church, came over with a couple bottles of wine. Nate and Elaine had also been at the house the night before, having learned from thirteen years in Central America the gift of simply being present with people in times of grief.

"You need to sleep tonight. We are here to help; we've brought medicine."

So, we laughed, cried, drank their holy wine . . . and that night, we did sleep.

Saturday morning a group of men helped me tear down the set for the show. Before we did, I took some pictures of the set, and another with Lee's costume on a stool beside the piano.

We loaded out and I pulled the light sliders down. The stage went dark, I turned off the board . . . and an instrument came on— an overhead light, directly where the stool with his costume had stood.

In the business, it's known as a "ghost light." It was to be the first of many "interesting occurrences."

When you're an extrovert and you have people around you, it's an odd and wonderful thing. Friday, Saturday, and Sunday were a flurry of activity. Ingrid and her friend Vandy came up from Florida, and they took charge of the video clips that we would show at the memorial service. My brother Tim and the rest of my family came down from Pennsylvania, and we put Tim in charge of the program design. My in-laws and my mom made food, and my father-in-law mowed the lawn. Later, I found out

Top: The *Jacob's Ladder* set. **Left:** Lee's costume. **Right:** Ghost light.

that my oldest son, Eliot, followed me around, picking up the pieces when I would forget to do whatever I said I would do, not letting me answer the phone, deflecting the calls from all over the country.

$$\P \quad \P \quad \P$$

Sunday afternoon was the viewing. By the time Sue and I and my folks arrived, a long line stretched out the front door. We went to the head of the line and became greeters, working our way back: friends from the road, Lee's relatives, Reagan's relatives, our relatives. Good friends from Goshen, Indiana, the Swartzentrubers, drove eleven hours for the viewing, then turned around and drove back home.

Monday afternoon. The memorial service was hectic: standing room only, with between nine hundred and one thousand people attending. At EMU's Lehman Auditorium the restrooms are downstairs. I was coming upstairs to the lobby when I saw two good friends and the college-age daughter of one of the friends. They had come in from Holland, Michigan, stayed for the funeral, and were leaving to go right back home. When I reached the top of the stairs and saw Bruce and John and John's daughter Jordan, I cried again.

If Lee had known the number of people he touched and who cared for him, would it have made a difference? Would he have listened? Would he have heard?

Or would the illness have drowned everything out, like it drowned out the voices of those closest to him—and his own cries?

$$\P \quad \P \quad \P$$

The memorial service was excruciating and amazing. I wrote and delivered a eulogy; it needed to be approached as just another performance. That "performance" was easier than the writing, when I needed to stop periodically and cry.

Eulogy of Lee Edward Eshleman

Ah, Lee. . . . Lee Edward Eshleman, that's L. E., not E. L., certainly not Eschleman, youngest son of Dr. J. Robert and Rosalie Eshleman, born August 28, 1963, in Richmond, Virginia, died May 17, 2007, at his home, 536 Hartman Drive, Harrisonburg, Virginia. He was forty-three years old.

He graduated from Eastern Mennonite High School, and from Eastern Mennonite University with a BA degree, an art major, with an English minor; the only class he didn't receive an A in . . . was an art class.

His wife, Reagan—whom he loved, respected, and looked up to—survives him. He depended on her, recognized her beauty and strength, agonized over whether he was good enough for her, called her remarkable. A son, Nicholas, with whom he shared a love of music, movies, and a sensitive nature. He so admired the boy Nick was, and the man he was becoming. A daughter, Sarah, with whom he shared a love of people. He was delighted by her physical ability, and her passion. We were pretty sure she would be running the company one day.

And Gabriel, age five, who astounded Lee with his insights, words, questions, and observations of life, nature, and with whom he loved to dissect frogs, snakes, and VCRs.

Also survived by an older brother, Curtis, his wife, Brigetta, three nieces, Hattie, Leena, and Althea. It was Curtis who was the adventuresome one, the one who got them into trouble.

He was a member of Community Mennonite Church; his last active participation was in an ensemble who sang all the names of the children in the congregation. The last name in the song was Gabe.

He was a partner in the company Ted & Lee TheaterWorks, a professional touring company based in Harrisonburg, Virginia. An actor, a writer, a props manager, a wares salesman, a graphic designer, web designer, businessman, and in all those roles, a purveyor of fine humor since 1987.

Lee, more than most, perhaps because much of his life was "more than most"—more height, more wit, more artistic ability, more sensitivity, more self-awareness, more pain—more than most, Lee was a man of paradoxes.

He was a great artist, both fine and graphic art, yet was color-blind. He was way better than he thought he was.

He was six foot four and not a basketball player.

A quicksilver wit who didn't like improv and, even more, didn't like change of any kind.

He was amazed by the grace of God, yet had to work so hard to feel it.

His stage presence was strong and commanding, full of strong choices, done in a great voice, yet was angered by his passivity in life, his own perceived weaknesses.

He was loving, considerate, and kind—yet he could be self-absorbed and selfish.

He loved puns, but had a one-of-a-kind understanding of the intricacies of humor and just how hard it could be.

A man of paradox.

He was a great Frisbee player, who loved The Guess Who, Elton John, Ellis Paul, Todd Snider, Paul McCartney, and The BoDeans.

He was a perfectionist.

He would eat anything.

But he loved bleu cheese dressing, mangoes, banana peppers, collard greens, Reuben sandwiches, and a good microbrew.

Picking out gifts was an excruciating experience. It involved making a decision . . . which was difficult: it involved possibly disappointing someone, which was paralyzing.

He loved comfortable jeans, pajamas, and big shirts with sleeves that were long enough.

He had an . . . uneven fashion sense.

If it fit and was comfortable, that was enough to put outfits together—and remember he *was* colorblind.

He might have had, in his words, the world's smallest bladder.

He also had perhaps the worst sense of direction in the Western world. We began to trust in his first instinct on which way to turn, and always go in the opposite direction.

He had great teeth, flossed every day, and looked really good in blue. He was a handsome man.

He loved to sleep in—he snored.

He was too often afraid.

He loved words, Dan Aykroyd, haikus, and speaking in Spanish.

He talked too loud on the cell phone. Listening to one-sided conversations during the dating years with Reagan was a sometimes disconcerting experience.

He hated to spend money.

He was an introvert, who needed his space away from people.

God, he was funny.

He forgave easily—he received forgiveness.

He was oh so exasperating.

He loved Jesus. He loved the stories of the church's grace, the church's love, and the church's charity; was greatly pained by stories of the church's intolerance, violence, and narrow-mindedness.

He loved wrapping laughter around magical moments of God's grace and presence. He also loved Squirrel Reunions and spews.

Last Sunday morning, in the last show we did, he once again played my brother.

The last lines he spoke on stage were, "Do you think there will be enough?" His last physical act on stage was a hug.

He was gifted greatly, flawed greatly, he was greatly human, he was greatly loved by God and by so many in the world.

He was Gabriel, he was Rudy, he was Andrew, he was Esau, Moses, Solomon, Marty, Uncle Laban, he was definitely Arnie Pufkin, he was Bill Brimley—host of Spew, the waiter at The Cathartic Café, he was a squirrel, a mole, a June bug. He was Nigel.

He was a lover of God, a child of God.

He was my best friend.

After the funeral Ingrid said, "Trent's here and some other singers—you should have a concert." We spread the word and talked to other musicians who were in town for the funeral, and at about seven o'clock that evening we started with drinks and food and music. Artists would rotate in, do two songs, then step back out: Ken Medema; George Baum and Michael Bridges of the group Lost and Found, Michael borrowing a guitar, George beating on a beer box; Brad Yoder; Herman Weaver; Trent Wagler (Trent premiered two songs that night, "Take Me Down to the River" and the completed "I Will Love You" inspired by the weekend); Chuck Neufeld; all backed by the electric guitar of Bart Reardon.

It was an amazing evening with great friends, great music, and their holy overlay of love and care. An evening of intense love and emotion, a raw gathering of grieving mourners, expressing the need to be together in song, tears, and laughter. An evening scalded into my memory—oddly, or perhaps not so oddly, one of my favorite events of all time.

The best God moments—when we are not aware of what we are doing.

Act 4

Falling Action

Wherein the falling action reveals the conflict between the protagonist and forces that challenge his resolve to continue the journey. Might contain a moment of final suspense, during which the final outcome is in doubt. May include severe weight loss.

SCENE 1

Scrambling for a Foothold

It WAS A NEW CHAPTER, one with even less of a map than trying to create a theater business out of nothing. When our family grocery business closed I vowed I would never again work with perishable goods. The thing about selling food is that it goes rancid or rots if you can't sell it. Sometimes I still wake up thinking: *That case of chicken breasts is going to go bad unless I do something with it right now.* Hardware doesn't work that way: if you buy a hammer, you may not return in a week to buy another one, but at least it won't go rancid.

So with the Ted & Lee business we sold ideas, performances, laughter—no perishable goods.

Unless someone dies.

Unless someone dies.

My language in normal conversation is "when Lee died," not "when Lee took his life" or "committed suicide." I feel that an apt description is, "Lee succumbed to a fatal illness known as depression."

Rock therapy

Late May, 2007. Our son Derek was home early for Lee's funeral after his first year of college. Standing in the backyard, I told him that Sue and I were thinking about creating a rock garden, in honor of Lee.

"Where do we get the rocks?"

"Construction sites in the area. It is Rockingham County, after all."

"What about that rock?" He was pointing to an embedded rock in the ground, a football-sized portion visible.

"We have no idea how big that is."

(Pause.)

"Can I dig it out?"

"We don't have any idea how large a rock it is. It may take days, weeks. We don't have the tools to get it out. Even if you dug it . . ."

(Pause.) He needed something to *do*, to drive his pain into something tangible.

"Sure, why not?"

So he started, with pick and shovel, to dig up this rock. After two weeks, he left for a month to work in a cannery in Alaska. The rock was not out yet. So I took up the pick and shovel, figuratively and literally. At least an hour a day, dirty, sweaty—because it felt good to do something physical, to not think, for at least that small space in time. After another two weeks of my picking and shoveling, our friend Dale Lehman brought his backhoe over, pulled the rock out and rolled it up to its final resting place, on the corner of our property.

The boys all dealt with the death of Lee in their own way—the beloved uncle—gone. Middle son Ian was in the Dominican Republic during the funeral, and the college he was attending discouraged him from coming home, a decision we all continue to regret. Later, Ian asked for a copy of the old Ted & Lee logo and made a tattoo out of it.

On the days that I believe, I will lift you up

For the summer of 2007, Lee and I had contracted to do five conferences. After his death, of course, we canceled all of those events. One of the clients, Church of the Nazarene, sent the entire fee anyway. Another, The Community of Christ, invited me, Sue, and anyone else I wanted to bring along to spend a week with them, all expenses paid. I asked Sue and my brother Tim to go.

The Community of Christ conference camp was one of our favorite places to perform. Travis Harder, Jamey Varvaro, Lisa Williams, Scott Giles, and others have become great friends. During our time there, Sue and I had lunch with Bart Campolo, one of the speakers. He asked me how I was doing, and I suppose I gave him a somewhat flippant answer. He spent the next hour figuratively kicking my ass, basically saying that if I didn't deal with the grief and the anger—if I kept stuffing it into a back room to deal with later—I *would*, not could, lose my significant relationships, including my marriage.

Bart does that to people. He's wonderfully kind and gentle—and brutally honest. At the end of his time at the camp, standing on the sidewalk, saying goodbye—Sue on my right, my brother Tim on my left—Bart said, "I won't tell you that I'll pray for you every day, because I don't do that even to my good friends, but on the days that I believe in God I will lift you up."

That phrase stuck in my head. The next summer, Trent Wagler and I began writing a play to premiere in October 2008, and that phrase was still in my head. I told this story to Trent, an amazing songwriter, and he did what artists do: he embraced the images, he felt the story in his soul and let it simmer, and then he let it out, with solo banjo.

If you have ears, you better hear me,
If you have eyes to see, (*once a cappella, then with banjo*)
Someday, someday, I will believe
Don't mistake me in what I say
I won't tell you that I'll pray, I won't tell you that I'll pray for you
But on the odd day that I believe,
I will give you to the air I breathe, I will hold you to the light I see
Someday, someday, I will believe
Do you see what I see, do you hear what I hear, do you feel the wind that's blowing?
If the stones aren't crying, and the fields aren't bleeding, what world is it you are seeing?
Someday, someday, I will believe
If you have ears, you better hear me,
If you have eyes to see,
Someday, someday, I will believe[41]

---

41 Trent Wagler, "Someday I Will Believe," 2008. Used by permission.

When I hear this song, it reminds me of Bart; it reminds me of those who stood beside me that day, Tim and Sue; and it reminds me of all those who stood beside me, all that year, holding me up.

Picking up pieces

A crisis in a business doesn't mean there isn't still work to be done. After Lee died, Abingdon Press called to say they still wanted to move forward on the video project. I was surprised but grateful; I was going to need the work it generated. So, two weeks after Lee's death, I began putting together the cast.

When I called an actor friend in California, his booming voice answered:

"Ted and Lee! (his caller ID said, "Ted & Lee TheaterWorks") Ted and Lee! I don't believe there is a Ted and Lee, because I never see or hear from Lee!!"

(Pause.)

"So you haven't heard?"

"What?"

"Lee took his life three weeks ago."

(Long, long pause.)

"I'm so sorry."

It happened over and over again as I heard from people around the country who had missed the news—and I would need to comfort their discomfort, brush off the faux pas they had just made.[42]

Coping and taking care of business

My first choice to play Andrew in *Fish-Eyes* was someone I had seen performing the role in another production, and performing it well. He said no. The second, a talented actor from Vancouver, said yes, and then two weeks later called to say that since he was not renewing his U.S. work visa, he had to decline.

---

42 In the fall of 2008 I performed segments of *Laughter and Lament*, a show I developed around my relationship with Lee. Before the benediction the worship leader referenced our history and impact, using our names three different times—however, he called me Lee. Despite the frantic waving of his wife he remained oblivious to his mistake. It continues to happen to this day.

Back to square one, or the drawing board, or whatever cliché is appropriate when life kicks you in the butt again. I decided to split the tasks: one actor for *Fish-Eyes*, and four actors, besides me, for *Creation Chronicles*, an eleven-character play.

Our third candidate for *Fish-Eyes* worked really hard on memorization, flew in on a Sunday, but by Monday night it was clear that it wasn't going to work. We had placed too many impossible obstacles in front of him. We had asked him to replace the actor—the one who had developed the character, cocreated the script, and performed beside his partner of twenty years—three months after he had taken his life. We had asked him to work with the remaining partner, the one with the haunted look in his eyes and the tendency to stare off into space.

Piece of cake.

I called Jason Hildebrand in Toronto—another Canadian who *did* have a U.S. work visa. I had met Jason at several conferences and festivals, including the one where I had missed a show due to the "severe contusion of my right forearm." He had been in the performers' meal tent, the only one in there who would talk to us, after members of the hot Christian rock band ignored us. Actors do need to stick together.

"Jason."

"Yeah?"

"I need an actor with big balls."

"And you thought of me?"

"Yeah."

"Thanks."

I flew up to Toronto and spent the weekend with him. We called it a dating weekend, seeing how we fit together, as best we could in two days.

A thought crossed my mind during this trip: after someone loses a spouse and starts dating, their children might ask furtively, "Isn't it a little soon for Daddy to be dating?"

Isn't it a little soon to be acting again—with anyone?

Jason jumped in and made the character his, with a different interpretation—a good thing. I was moving at 60 to 70 percent; I got the words right, I got the movements right, but the inner light, the fun, was elusive. Finally in the last dress rehearsal for the video shoot, a trickle of the old magic, the old fun, began to run. It was like brushing off the dirt from a trail marker and finding my way again.

The Abingdon Press project included filming *Fish-Eyes* and *Creation Chronicles*, the two shows I had written with Lee, created our identity around, and performed thousands of times. Rehearsing them was painful and life-giving at the same time. The constant flow of people through our house and the theater was what I needed to keep going, but the ghost of Lee's performances of this material was floating above each shot.

Once during lunch someone asked, "How are you doing this?"

All I could think was, "You compartmentalize everything."

The video shoots that fall kept me moving, surrounded by caring, talented people, adrenalin replacing grieving, work replacing reflection. It was a little like taking a rancid piece of meat and, rather than disposing of it, just tucking it behind the couch and hoping the smell goes away. I had a sneaking suspicion that not dealing with pain in the moment was not a good idea.

❡ ❡ ❡

Acting during this period was familiar, comforting, and excruciating at the same time. Trying to write comedy was strange; I wasn't exactly sure if I was still funny.

One of the scenes we shot was the final scene from *Live at Jacob's Ladder*, where Jacob returns home and asks forgiveness for stealing the birthright and blessing that rightfully belonged to Esau. It was the climax of the show Jeff, Lee, and I were to perform May 18, the day after Lee died.

ESAU: You've done a good job of trying to bribe me into coming home, but I don't ever recall you asking me to forgive you.

(*silence*)

ESAU: Why is that so hard for you, to ask?

JACOB: It can't be that easy.

ESAU: Who said it was easy?

JACOB: All right Esau, will you forgive me?

Curt Cloninger, an actor friend from Atlanta, was playing Esau and I was playing Jacob. Ingrid was directing, and she said we were fine in the scene. When a director says you're fine, you are in trouble. There didn't seem to be anything in the reserve tank. We weren't swapping molecules. Honesty was missing. Ing's idea: "What if it was Lee coming back, asking for forgiveness? What would that feel like? To be on the receiving end of the question 'Will you forgive me?'"

That unlocked something inside of me, and the scene finally had life. I wondered how the group of high school students, quietly observing from the back of the auditorium, felt about the general spilling of vital organs out on the stage like that.

Heroes come in different shapes and sizes. Through the fall of 2007 people were holding me up, pointing me in the right direction when my eyes would glaze over, much like 1993 in Philadelphia when Joy or Sue would say, "turn right" when Lee and I would emerge out of the hotel, blinking and dazed in the sunlight.

Old friends Bob Small and Kathleen Tosco hosted the company in Plainwell, Michigan, while Bob did the initial directing of the video material.

Ingrid directed and dramaturged the Abingdon video shoots on-site, guiding the actors through difficult steps of performing in the shadow of loss. She also performed with me in several Ted & Lee contracts, in one case stepping in and portraying Andrew in a *Fish-Eyes* show. We dressed her in a mushroom hat and long jacket—she looked like an adorable newsboy.

Agent Sheri Hartzler picked through the shambles of the business and guided it through the complexity of an enterprise that had lost half its staff and half its life. She now took over the product department and script oversight. She also produced the huge undertaking of the three video shoots, all while trying to convince a public they should still book this theater company, the one limping. There were months I simply couldn't pay her and she soldiered on, all while negotiating her own grief. She too had lost a great friend and coworker.

Sheri, in her other job, had recently produced two videos on grief and suicide, and so became a great source of information and grace for many around her. I will be ever grateful for her strength and resolve.

Lee's wife Reagan was the other person in the world who best understood the emotions of that fall, the loss of the other half; we joked about each being the "other" spouse, the one who had the inside stories.

Sue was a rock of strength and love for the years of "fog wandering" in anger and grief. It is no surprise that she worked through her own grief and mourning with self-care and readings, her organizational mind leading her to the most effective process of healing. She also gave me the space to flounder and flail, without ever judging my choice to remain in theater, even through the years of diminished income.

Who is this guy?

There were moments when I didn't recognize this person I had become. I was angry with myself—that Lee's death had altered me so much, that I cared that much, that I was that vulnerable. Several times that fall I used the phrase, "You might have to excuse me, I don't know if it's the grief or if I'm just an asshole today."

I wanted people to cut me a break, but at the same time not treat me any differently—a double bind I was to subject people to, over and over again.

I continue to be amazed at the impact Lee's death had. Any sudden death would have such an impact, but a suicide—of a performer whose job was to affect audiences emotionally—seemed to touch people in ways that seemed disproportionate. I've gradually become more aware of the dynamic around celebrity and public personas. Because actors and other performing artists allow people inside their lives and personalities, we feel we have come to know them. People felt they knew Lee, if in fact they knew only a portion of him. It was like losing a close friend.

Years later, friend Sam P. put it this way: "The two of you got in here"—put his hand on his chest—"and then when he died, we didn't have any way to deal with it—you bastards."

Another friend, John Y. said, "I should have been at the memorial service . . . I was hung over . . . a bunch of us got together, just to talk about Lee . . . bourbon was there. I'm sorry I wasn't there."

My reply: "Maybe you should just call it an early wake and stop beating yourself up."

DoveTale 2007

Whether or not it was a good idea, we decided to keep the show contracts already booked before Lee's death and actively pursue others. The *DoveTale* tour of December 2007 was an eleven-show tour—one of which was fun. The others varied from workmanlike to painful.

Trent Wagler stepped in and did a wonderful job, as both Ingrid and I worked through our own grief. Trent's Gabriel was different, of course; his innocence and playfulness, along with his musical ability, made his interpretation unique. It's a very difficult task to replace an actor in a live production. Years later I still don't know if it was a good idea. Let's just file the experience under the flailing of a floundering surviving partner—one more thing I don't know.

We had also shot *DoveTale* for video in January of 2007. Lee was a whirlwind in prep for the shoot, designing the set along with Jeff Warner, painting and creating props. The shoot went well, and it was after this intense activity ended that he seemed to drift downward.

At the time of Lee's death in May, the editing and production of the final DVD wasn't finished. We pushed forward on the editing.

Old friend Wayne Gehman heroically volunteered his time, spending hours in the editing room, watching his good friend Lee over and over again to have production ready for the winter's tour. We rushed production for the *DoveTale* tour in December. The sales were disappointing during that tour; it seems people either wanted the version they had just seen with Trent or weren't interested.

Another defeat in a year of loss.

SCENE 2

The Protagonist Loses His A** and Most of His Mind

I WAS CROUCHED at the foot of the stage in Murfreesboro, Tennessee, Easter Sunday 2008. Above me were 183 yellow T-shirt clad kids lip-syncing a song about Jesus. I was barefoot, the floor was cold, I was trying to find the familiar rush of adrenaline before a performance. I was with Jason. We were getting ready to perform pieces of *Fish-Eyes*: "Arrest and Denial" and "Breakfast on the Shore."

"Breakfast," the last piece Lee and I had performed together.

And it hit me: *I can't do this anymore.*

The toxic stuff that I had stuffed inside was driving the art and joy out of my body and soul. It really felt right to say, finally, "No more. I can't say these lines, make these moves, feel the emotions of the scenes—can't do it anymore." Once I verbalized this decision, I was shocked by the relief I felt, which in turn was immediately followed by emptiness.

So, was *this* to be the last time that I would perform these scenes? Here, in a basketball arena in front of people still filing in for an Easter service, following dancing kids lip-syncing songs about Jesus? It was overwhelmingly depressing.

We stepped onstage, began the familiar steps into a scene I had performed over a thousand times with Lee but just four previous times with Jason. An actor has to claim the space onstage and make it his or her own; familiar movements and blocking help an actor relax into the moment.

In a space this large you are primarily acting for the camera. I hit my mark for camera four as we had rehearsed, and just as I spoke—"Andrew, what are all those soldiers doing here?"—the fire alarm went off.

In a basketball arena that seats twelve thousand, that's a real healthy fire alarm. Of course we stopped and waited. The moment was obviously ruined. It's difficult enough to act in a real theater space, let alone a basketball arena—but when you add a pulsing alarm it becomes surreal. No one was going with us on this one— all semblance of suspension of disbelief was as long gone as the devil was in Georgia.

The fire marshal was the only one who could turn off the alarm; he was not in the building, but rather "on his way." However, we were on a tight schedule, and so the lead pastor waved at us to continue.

Continue? Really?

Yes, yes!!

Okay. We plowed right on, shouting now, trying to find any kind of nuance to our lines.

Me proclaiming, as Peter, "I don't know this man! I wouldn't be caught dead with him!" Playing to the cameras that transfer to the big screen, half the five thousand still filing in, the pulsing screech of the alarm not *quite* becoming background noise. It seemed a bizarre ending to the play that had taken Lee and me across the country and parts of the world.

We finished that memorable set and then, during the rest of the service, while the choir sang and special guest Charlie Daniels did his set, I thought to myself, *You really haven't experienced Easter until you've heard the original "Devil Went Down to Georgia." Nothing says "He is risen" like fast fiddle and "My name is Johnny, and I'm the best that's ever been."*

Jason and I agreed we wouldn't perform *Fish-Eyes* again. It simply hurt too much to perform the one show that still was our most recognized product.

Jason: "Just take six or eight months off, ride your bike, work around the house, clear your head."

When I broached the subject with Sue on the ride home, she was not as wild about the idea. Instead of asking her folks if we could suspend mortgage payments for those months, she was hoping to accelerate. I clammed up, and from there I started a long descent into the depression I had long expected and somehow put off until then.

Easter Sunday 2008. He is risen indeed.

Earlier that week I had started a cleansing raw-foods diet. It was touted to clean you out, mind and body—I sure could use both of those. I jumped right in, juicing vegetables, eating no cooked food, salads every night. I could get a handle on this, this I could do. I found out later it was classic anorexic behavior: *If I can't control other aspects of my life, I can at least control what goes in my body.*

I began riding bike an hour a day as well. I started to feel better physically, at least; at about four weeks the pounds started melting off. It now became a game: How much could I lose? Fifteen pounds, twenty . . . that's where I would stop. Probably should stop. Nope, twenty-five . . . nope. Final total: thirty-two pounds lost. I was wearing the same two pairs of jeans, the only ones that fit, over and over again; rotating them around washdays.

That fall, Ingrid and I did a show on a Saturday night, and then Sunday morning participated in a worship service where I did a children's story. On the way to our next gig:

Ing: "Can I tell you something?"

"Sure."

"When you were up front, doing the children's story?"

"Right."

"You kept touching your butt."

"I did?"

"Yes."

"Wow."

"It was as if you were convincing yourself it was really gone."

"Well, that's embarrassing."

"Well . . . yeah, for all of us."

I reached 169 pounds. I felt better—at least physically. I found out later that a number of people were convinced I had cancer. *Wouldn't that be a real shame, first Lee, now Ted (sigh). At least we have the videos.*

❥ ❥ ❥

Part of what happened when Lee died was that he took the inventory with him; he took the brand with him.

A friend writing a doctoral dissertation on vaudeville of the early twentieth century told me that when a longtime vaudeville team lost a member—either through retirement or death—the surviving member almost never got a steady partner, but instead either joined a larger company, went solo, or quit. When performing artists begin young, defining themselves as artists together, it can feel as if their identities are irrevocably forged together. For another person to fill that role is too painful.

Lee and I began working together when he was twenty-three and I was thirty—and the excitement and joy we felt at "doing a show" or writing pieces together could never be replicated. When it made us laugh in the office, we knew it would work onstage. It was our unfailing barometer: if it cracked us up, it went in the show.

I remember so distinctly when we moved from doing sketches here and there to being asked to "put on a show." Walking back to the hotel room at the camp where we performed in 1990, I found myself thinking, *We just did a show. Like real actors. It had a beginning, middle and end . . . wow. Maybe, maybe there is something here.* I also remember thinking so clearly, *We can make this work, because Lee is so good.*

It was about that same time, around 1992, that Barbra Graber asked me if I was prepared for what would happen when Lee left. She assumed because he was so good someone would snap him up, or he'd move to L.A., or . . . or . . .

Hmm, I wonder if she asked Lee what he would do if I left.

On a road trip one December in the early 2000s, I was lying down on the back seat trying to sleep while Lee and Ingrid were in the front. They were discussing the business, the company, and his and my relationship. I heard Lee say, "He better not die, because I don't know what I would do if he did."

"Das Flassen" was a sketch where Lee sang an opera in an indeterminate language—"a rare Nordic tongue"—while I translated using large cards, "in order to preserve the silent tone." My translation turns into a critique of the song, then Lee's performance, and then Lee himself. Lee gave a great "explanation" to the audience regarding the conflict around the sketch, my reluctance to do it at all, his insistence. His lines:

```
I know Ted didn't want to do this piece, but
I thought we were ready to bring something
special . . . and ahmm, Ted usually makes
these final decisions, because . . . well . . .
he's older . . . considerably older.

But one day he's gonna die, and when that
happens, where am I gonna be? . . . and so I
thought today . . . today would be the day I
could soar like the eagles, but instead, I
plummeted, like a cast-iron egret. I'm sorry
I let you good people down; this isn't the
first time . . . sometimes I think it would be
better if it was just Ted and . . .
```

One day, he's gonna die.

❡ ❡ ❡

To this day, I have no desire to acquire a steady acting, writing, or business partner. I have enjoyed growing as an artist with all the actors and writers I have worked with since 2007, but it feels untenable to "replace" Lee.

However, I found myself getting angry with people who assumed that without Lee I couldn't go on. I was asked if I would go back to school or teach. Or enter the pastorate. *What a great move that would have been. Take a wounded, angry man and put him in charge of a congregation.*

I guess it was a moment of defiant rage for me to say:

I don't need Lee to remain in this business.

I don't need Lee to still be an actor.

I don't need Lee to still be a writer.

What Would Lloyd Do?

What Would Lloyd Do? was the fourth play I had written or cowritten in 2008, in the months between February and October. Before a play even premiered, I was beginning the work on the next one, trying to stay busy, trying to recreate a business from the ground up. Trying to stay creative while sliding into the deepest depression I've ever experienced.

What Would Lloyd Do? is the story of a fifty-two-year-old pastor—burned out, angry, estranged from family. Mike is separated from his wife, but follows her from the Philadelphia suburbs to Cincinnati, Ohio, to be near his children, where the only job he finds is with a struggling inner city church propped up by an endowment. This endowment only continues as long as the Sunday morning services are broadcast on radio, a vestige of the largess of the late Lloyd, a past member of the congregation. No one attends any longer and Jeff, the young bar singer he hires (a music director is also in the bylaws) is dumfounded by the resolve to go through the motions of church just for a job. Their tenuous relationship comes to a boil one Sunday morning right before broadcast time, when Jeff challenges Mike to finally preach something honest.

```
JEFF: At least I'm trying to do something . . .
I don't see you trying to do anything . . .
anything real. Where's the guy who locked me
out of the office, that was—where's the guy
who shot the organ? I liked that guy—that guy
```

didn't care about rocking the boat. He knew
this wasn't working . . . Okay, why don't
you tell me something I would actually care
about; something I've never heard a hundred
times before—I'm going out here—one person,
in an empty space . . . now there's some-
body out here—why should I listen? What do
you have? It's Elijah today right? What about
Elijah? I dare you, I dare you.

Just before Mike blows up at the singer, sound tech Doug flips
the "On Air" switch and for the first time since his move, Mike
broadcasts something honest. A portion of that sermon allowed
me to rage against God, circumstances, and the church:

MIKE: Elijah! . . . Elijah went to Mount
Horeb, the mountain of God, where he spent
the night. The Lord came to him and said,
"What are you doing here?"

Elijah answered, "I've always obeyed you. But
your people have broken promises, torn down
your altars and killed all your prophets,
except me. And now they are trying to get me."

"Go out and stand on the mountain," the Lord
replied. "I want you to see me when I pass
by."

All at once, a strong wind shook the mountain
and shattered the rocks. But the Lord was not
in the wind. Next, there was an earthquake,
but the Lord was not in the earthquake. Then
there was a fire, but the Lord was not in the
fire.

Where do we find God? Is he ever where we
expect, or where we need . . . how do we
know? It's as if . . .

(*suddenly take a pose*)

. . . you're on the mound, on the pitcher's
mound—peering in to home plate for the signal—looking for which pitch to use—a fast-
ball? a curve ball? . . . the signal that
comes in from the coach—we trust the coach
right?

(*He takes the pose of a pitcher getting the
signal from the catcher.*)

—Is God in the wind?

(*shakes head*)

No . . . Is God in the earthquake—big splash,
the earthquake . . . but . . .

(*shakes head*)

No . . . Is God in the fire? He's done that
before—he's a big fan of fire . . . but . . .
no. God is in . . .

(*nods to the "catcher"*)

. . . the silence.

(*He completes his windup and delivers the
"pitch"—it's creamed over the fence.*)

Oh no, the pitch is hammered, is not God
in the silence??? I thought God was in the
silence.

(*checks the text*)

It must be me . . . The Bible says so, right?
The Bible is not wrong . . .

(*this time through twice as fast*)

Is God in the wind?

(*shakes head*)

No. Is God in the earthquake—

(*shakes head*)

No, is God in the fire?—he's a big fan of fire
. . . but . . . no. God is in . . .

(*nods to the "catcher"*)

. . . the silence.

(*He completes his windup and delivers the
"pitch"—it's creamed over the fence.*)

It appears as if God is not in the silence
. . . He's not here!!! I'm confused . . . I'm
listening, I'm . . .

(*pause to effect*)

. . . silent.

I hear nothing. We want a God who loves us
. . . guides our steps along the way. You
pray it will be so . . . there's a reason for
everything. But bad stuff keeps happening!
How is God here—in the neighborhoods where
you're afraid to walk outside after seven
o'clock? Where schools are crumbling
. . . where . . . you can't pull yourself up,
because there's nothing to grab on to . . .
When marriages and families fall apart . . .
It seems when we need God the most . . . when
I need God the most . . . I can't hear God.
What does that mean? Does it mean he hears
but can't do anything . . . or he doesn't
care? He hears but won't do anything? Which
is it ? . . . Am I asking too much? Where is
God? Is God in the wind? Is God in the fire? I
keep listening . . . I keep listening.

The change in my weight, coupled with the depression, created someone I no longer recognized. The space I was taking up—or more accurately, not taking up—was both physical and mental. I was avoiding people, shrinking into myself. I felt small, unable to affect the world around me.

Laurelville 2008

One of the pieces I wrote for the Abingdon video shoot in the fall of 2007 was based on the book of Revelation; the whole book in eight minutes. The process of getting the monologue on its feet was an example of art as a communal effort.

I first contacted a local scholar, Duane Yoder, who sat with me over two ninety-minute sessions working through the book—what was important, what wasn't. What was understandable; what did any of this mean? I loved one of his lines: "This section? Don't bother with that—no one knows what that means."

I wrote a version I wasn't terribly happy with, again working with Bob Small as dramaturge. During a discussion of this bizarre scripture Bob said, "It sounds like it's a piece Zeus would do." Zeus was a character I had created when we first worked together back in 1992 on the *Armadillo Tour*.

Zeus's voice was grating and low. He wore a long coat, fingerless gloves, a knit cap, and had a peculiar warped, but somehow profound, viewpoint on life. I had grown to love Zeus. He gave me an avenue to speak in a voice even more slightly off-center.

Giving the scene to Zeus changed the entire piece. It made so much sense for Revelation to be seen through the eyes of this man. When I brought the scene to rehearsal, Ingrid activated it, pushing to find the physical elements and actions, while saxophonist Brad Yoder added an eerie live soundtrack. And the piece worked. The last part of the monologue:

```
And then there was music, harps and 144,000
singin' in a choir—whoa, at's a big choir.
The angels bring judgment on those that wor-
ship the beast—but the saints are faithful to
Jesus—Jesus, I know him, we have coffee on
42nd street every Tuesday morning; sometimes
he buys, sometimes he lets me buy. 'Nen there
was a woman . . . a woman dressed in sunlight
and she was ready to give birth—but there was
a dragon . . . ready to eat the child . . .
but Michael—I had a cousin named Michael,
he's a dancer—Michael and the rest of the
angels in heaven fought the dragon . . . and
the battle was won . . . the battle is won
. . . the battle is won. . . . I saw a new
heaven and a new earth. . . . a new Jerusa-
lem, a holy city. I heard a loud voice shout
from the throne: "God's home is now with
his people. He will live with them, and they
will be his own. He will wipe all tears from
their eyes, and there will be no more death,
suffering, crying, or pain. These things of
the past are gone forever." Yeah, John, that
sounds about right . . . Don't be afraid . . .
Don't be afraid . . . Don't be afraid . . .

END OF SCENE.
```

The next time I performed this piece was at a worship and music weekend at Laurelville Mennonite Church Center in Pennsylvania. I was a resource person for the retreat, and the presenters were to introduce themselves in a creative way. I decided to perform Revelation. Most in the group knew Ted & Lee, and for many it was the first time they had seen me since Lee's death.

Actors should always be aware of their audience, but I missed on this one. When I finished, there was no applause, no sounds of appreciation at all. Being an actor and consequently thinking I had performed badly, I was confused. We sat, seconds ticked by, and it finally hit me. The words from the last phrases of the piece echoed in my head: "there will be no more death, suffering, crying, or pain. These things of the past are gone forever."

They had watched me with the absence of Lee on their minds, and consequently heard this piece differently than I perhaps intended. And then, so did I. It was a profound moment of illumination for me. The writing I was doing was shaped in huge ways by the loss and grief; all the major characters I wrote during those two years found themselves imbued with loss, pain, and a journey through grief.

Counseling might have been cheaper.

Growing old with Lee

We thought—or at least I thought—we would grow old together onstage. In informal settings, or in workshops when people would ask us about our future or question our relationship, I assumed Lee and I would always be a duo in much the same way I assume Sue and I will always be a couple. There was so much more we could have done.

We joked that we would be performing the play *Fish-Eyes* until we died. It would be like Led Zeppelin performing "Stairway to Heaven" when they are eighty, or The Who singing "My Generation" from wheelchairs.

We improv-ed a scenario where we would do *Fish-Eyes* at eighty-five and seventy-eight, respectively. Each scene would have us shuffling into position, squinting into the light. For example, Peter and Andrew in "The Feeding of the 5,000," referring to Jesus:

"Does he know what time it is?"

(Pause.)

"What?"

"I said, does he know what time it is?"

"I don't know—how long's he been talking?"

(Pause.)

"What?"

"I said, I don't know! How long's he been talking?!"

"Three days."

"What?"

"Three days!"

(Long pause.)

At which point we would just wave in annoyance: "Ahhhhhh." We would turn away and shuffle back offstage. And the scene would be over.

Next scene:

"Would you just look at this place?"

(Pause.)

"What?"

"Would you just look at this place? This is no place to have a dinner."

"What?"

"I said, this is no place to have a dinner!"

And so on, each time waving in annoyance to signify premature ending of the scene. Each scene would last no more than four or five lines, and would always include "What?!"—the result of two actors whose hearing is 70 percent gone. I figure we could have done the entire ninety-minute show in seven and a half minutes. Just in time to be in bed by eight following the seven o'clock show.

Just one more bit I don't get to do at parties anymore.

❡ ❡ ❡

In April of 2007, a month before Lee died, we were in Georgia with a good friend, Curt Cloninger. We were performing in his hometown, and he joined us for lunch and stayed for the show. One of his comments stuck with me: "I'm jealous of having someone with whom there are so many inside jokes."

It's one thing to lose a whole repertoire of performance material; it's yet another to lose twenty years of memories, twenty years of creative minds always looking for the comedy button to push, the one that was unique with your relationship.

Future audiences won't be able to watch Lee continue to grow as a performer. What would we have created together next? To this day, it is when I handle costumes and props that were exclusively Lee's that I feel the most loss and sadness. It's the tactical, the bodily remembering, that affects me the most. I can talk about him, the suicide, the loss, but picking up Nigel's sweater or Gabriel's overalls drives right into me.

In the last three years I have had recurring dreams of being on the road with Lee, most with a very vivid component. In almost every occasion, we are both aware that he is gone and that he took his own life. In one I dreamed that he had simply been hiding. When he showed up, I was frantic:

"You know we thought you were dead?!"

"Yes."

"We had a funeral!"

"I saw it."

"You saw it?!"

"Yeah."

In the dream I was now brainstorming a plan to reveal to the world he was still alive. How would he fit into the business? Would he replace an actor, with whom I had cowritten a different show?

Would we go back to performing Ted & Lee shows? I was grateful he was alive, but confused about what it meant.

In another, Lee looked at me as we were packing up after a show and congratulated me on the new projects I was working on. I said, "It would be more fun if I were doing them with you."

He said, "Then you should have done more to help me."

My response: "Is that why you gave me the ultimate middle finger?"

End of dream.

Growing up with God

I used to joke that I was raised a Mennonite who's also a middle child, so I don't expect much. I always felt God was more interested in what we could do for others than what we ourselves needed. So I didn't ask for much, because getting things wasn't what my relationship with God was based on. When Lee died, it manifested itself in this way: *What right do I have? Why would God deal with my pain, my sense of profound loss and growing depression, when God wouldn't heal Lee?* Rather than seeing God as a place to discover a connection and healing, I chose—and in many ways, still choose—to remove myself from God. Do I hold God responsible?

In the months following Lee's death, my own anger and guilt led me toward a dismissal of a God who wouldn't heal my best friend.

The next spring Jeff Raught asked me, "So how are you with God?"

As artists, sometimes we think too much in our particular medium: when you are a writer, you hear dialogue around you all the time; when you are an actor you should be in constant observation of the interaction you see. I felt like I was writing a script.

My answer was, "Me and God aren't talking right now."

Jeff's response: "But he's still listening."

It was an interesting idea. So I put it into a play: *Tattered and Worn*.

In the play the homeless man Zeus is visited by a piano-playing angel, Jeff, who brings with him a trunk full of props. The angel

Gabriel tricks Zeus into rooting through the trunk and recreating scenes from plays he wrote and performed in a past life. Over the course of the play Zeus realizes he has lost his acting partner to death and this is the reason he has lost his faith and his way.

Healing is about "getting back in the boat" and voyaging through the stages of grief and loss.

It is an amazing paradox. We are made with wonderful capacities to love. We need to be loved, and—just as importantly—we need *to* love. At the same time, we are created so fragile—both mentally and physically fragile. It seems unfair, then, to know we are set up to experience profound loss. We all have the potential to become experts on grief.

But we also are capable of holding one another up. In the last scene of *What Would Lloyd Do?*, Mike returns to the church on a Sunday morning with this "sermon":

```
The prophet Habakkuk . . . Habakkuk saw a
world filled with pain, filled with violence
. . . but he also saw a choir . . . he heard
music. This morning I went to the park. I
didn't hear anything. I listened . . . I lis-
tened for God . . . but there was silence.
And then in the silence I heard a runner
. . . I heard a train in the distance . . .
I heard birds . . . I heard children. I heard
anger . . . I heard laughter. I heard a city
waking up . . . in the distance I heard music.

In this life there is grace, but never
enough. There is peace, but never enough.
There is love . . . but never enough.

I am disappointed. I'm disappointed in
myself, I'm disappointed in God . . . I don't
come to you healed this morning . . . I
```

don't come to you with answers to any questions. But I choose to be here, here where
the unhealed gather . . . So we take what we
have, we break it, and we pass it out.

I choose to be here, in this place. I choose
to walk with you . . . to drink from the cup
with you.

And so, for those of us whose journeys aren't yet over, we continue to grow.

In this life there is grace . . . but is it enough?

There is peace . . . but is it enough?

There is love . . . but is it enough?

We take what we have . . . which is never enough . . . we break
it, and we pass it out.

Act 5

Dénouement

Wherein the conflicts are resolved. May include a revelation of the protagonist's reaction to the struggle within earlier acts.

Wall
could be extended this way.

A Path Back

I DON'T TRULY KNOW how healing works. I don't know if I can truly claim healing. I *do* know that without writing and acting, without continuing to work by sheer, naive persistence—I can't envision any type of healing. It has meant getting up and moving, doing the only thing I felt equipped to do: write and act. Each new project I started after Lee's death was both an act of defiance and an act of desperation. Almost twenty-five years ago theater was my path into a sense of being. Now it's the way back.

A path can also be a marked trail, evidence of having been this way before. But only if we recognize the small moments that mark our journey, the ones that show where we have come from and the path ahead.

December 2010. I am standing backstage at Ridgeview Mennonite Church, Gordonville, Pennsylvania, taking deep breaths, clearing my head, waiting for my cue. Listening to Jeff Raught's fingers flying on the piano, while he's hunched over the keys. In truth, Jeff doesn't merely play the piano—he has an intimate relationship with the keyboard.

My cue is the last strains of the opening song for our show *Just Give 'Em the News*. In a flash, I think about the first time Jeff and I met. Ingrid, Lee, and I were doing *DoveTale* at Ridgeview, and Jeff played pre-show music. Lee was a huge fan of Jeff's selections, including Vince Guaraldi's "Linus and Lucy" music from the *Peanuts* specials.

Waiting backstage—a place millions of people all over the world have stood. Some nervous, some calm, others with dread or excitement or profound thankfulness for the opportunity to exercise gift and craft. Millions have gone through this ritual, hundreds of millions of times. Some get physically ill, to the point of throwing up. Most of us have a rush of adrenaline that heightens awareness and pushes our pulse up. It's the body taking care of us, once again.

Every rehearsal, every script read, every class, every line reading, every *aha* moment when you "get it," every spot where the audience gasps, laughs, or cries, or even falls asleep, every acting partner—Steve, Christian, Sharon, Cami, Christy, Janice, Nick R., Nick M., Colby, Craig, Mel, Andi, Lee B., Jeremy, Pam, Duane, Joy, Tim R., Kirk, Cori, Suzanne, Pete V., Rich, Kevin, Chris, Madeline, Curt, McNair, Jason H., Robin, Sara, Pete, Deb, Braydon, Heidi, Charley, Tyler, Quill. And those who have shared the road and the stage: Jeff, Trent, Jay, Ingrid, Ken M., Tim, and especially Lee . . .

It's live theater, and there is nothing like it.

Every line you've uttered, every gesture you've made, every mistake, every pickup of a dropped line, every missed cue, every kiss, every fall, every entrance and exit, every pause while you let the audience feel and use their imagination, every silence when you expected a laugh, every standing ovation—every moment you have committed to this life and this art is here.

Every doubt when the character seemed elusive, every crying baby in the audience, every desperate lunge of a graceless attempt at dance, every tedious road trip, missed flight, 3:30 a.m. wake-up call, every sound check, every prayer for energy—a wide-open life of wonder.

Each one of these moments, each one of these teachers, actors, writers, and friends has had a hand in bringing me to this moment, and I am profoundly grateful.

The Final Story

Tattered and Worn with musician/composer Jeff Raught.

Excellent Trouble with Ingrid De Sanctis.

What's So Funny about Money? with Jeff Raught.

What Would Lloyd Do? with musician/composer Trent Wagler and Jay Lapp.

St. John's Revival and Music Review with musician/composer Trent Wagler.

I'd Like to Buy an Enemy
with Tim Ruebke.

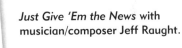

Just Give 'Em the News with
musician/composer Jeff Raught.

Timeline

Major and minor hits of Ted & Lee TheaterWorks,
followed by the Ted & Company TheaterWorks

Fall of 1987
    First comedy sketches
Summer of 1991
    Akimbo formed
Summer of 1992
    First full-length show, *Ted & Lee Live: The Armadillo Tour.*
        Pieces included "Looks at Books," "Meat Shoppe,"
        "When Shrimp Learn to Whistle," "Bus Stop," "Spew!"
Spring of 1994
    *Fish-Eyes: Stories You Thought You Knew Through the Eyes of
        the Disciples*
Fall of 1997
    Creation Chronicles
Fall and Winter of 1997
    DoveTale with Ingrid De Sanctis
Spring of 2003
    The Bob Show
Fall of 2005
    Live at Jacob's Ladder with musician/composer Ken Medema
May of 2007
    Lee's death

Fall of 2007
  Writing for video: *The Big Story* video

Spring of 2008
  Tattered and Worn with musician/composer Jeff Raught
  Excellent Trouble with Ingrid De Sanctis

Summer of 2008
  What's So Funny about Money? First version with musician/
    composer Trent Wagler

Fall of 2008
  What Would Lloyd Do? with musician/composer Trent Wagler

January of 2009
  Paul: Did You Get the Letter I Sent?

Spring and Summer of 2009
  I'd Like to Buy an Enemy
  *Speak Up, I Can't Hear Your Life: All of Church History in 90
    Minutes*
  St. John's Revival and Music Review with musician/composer
    Trent Wagler

Fall of 2009
  The Big Story: The Entire Bible in 80 Minutes
  Just Give 'Em the News with musician/composer Jeff Raught

Fall of 2010
  Laughter and Lament

Acknowledgments

Great thanks to Mom and Dad, Robert and Ruth Swartz, for saying "write whatever you want," finding the old photos, and living lives of faith and authenticity.

To my siblings and best friends, Tim Swartz and Tina Swartz Burkholder, for *their* sides of the story; for unconditional love and friendship; for allowing me the comfortable middle spot.

To Sheri Hartzler for years of support.

To Reagan Eshleman for sharing the stories and for permission to use Lee's line drawings.

To MennoMedia staff: Amy Gingerich for asking, "Do you think you'd like to write a book?" and Byron Rempel-Burkholder for shepherding the work with patience and good humor.

To preliminary readers: Shirley Showalter, Arlyn Friesen Epp, Ingrid De Sanctis, and especially Dan Hess.

Special thanks to Jim Clemens, who made the early manuscript look intelligible and kept asking, "Book?"

Making Mennos Laugh Since 1987.

The Author

Ted Swartz is a playwright and actor who has been mucking around in the worlds of the sacred and profane for more than twenty years. Ted fell in love with acting and theater on his way to a traditional pastorate in the Mennonite church, a denomination not usually thought of as a hotbed of theatrical opportunities.

Coupling theater and seminary education, Ted became a theologian of a different sort. He discovered that at the intersection of humor and biblical story we often find new or different understandings of scripture.

Ted's love of acting, comedy, and collaboration with creative partner Lee Eshleman took him to performances in forty-five states in the U.S., Canada, as well as shows in Kenya and Japan. Ted & Lee became known for a quirky and gently askew view of life, building a loyal following.

Despite the tragic loss of Lee to suicide in 2007, Ted continued the search for the intersection of comedy and faith, grief and loss, deepening that exploration.

He is the creator or co-creator of over a dozen plays, and continues to perform and write across the U.S. and abroad. Born in Phoenixville, Pennsylvania, Ted is a 1989 graduate of Eastern Mennonite University and 1992 grad of Eastern Mennonite Seminary.

Ted now lives in the Shenandoah Valley of Virginia. Along with writing and acting, his loves include his wife, Sue; three sons, Eliot, Ian, and Derek; daughters-in-law, Katrina, Hannah, and Chelsea;

and newest addition, granddaughter Mona Quinn.

He and Sue are members of Community Mennonite Church in Harrisonburg, Virginia.

Find more at www.TedandCompany.com or www.MennoMedia.org/Ted.